The Man
Who Would Preach

Robert E. Keighton

ABINGDON PRESS

NEW YORK • NASHVILLE

THE MAN WHO WOULD PREACH

Copyright © MCMLVI by Pierce & Washabaugh

The Epilogue "I Am a Minister" was first
published in *Crozer Quarterly* and is copyright 1948 by Crozer Theological Seminary.

SET UP, PRINTED, AND BOUND BY THE
PARTHENON PRESS, AT NASHVILLE,
TENNESSEE, UNITED STATES OF AMERICA

To

G.E.K.

In appreciation as well as gratitude,
for memory as well as hope

Foreword

The minister has several texts that he can call upon to maintain his place in the ministry. As one who serves the people he recalls, "The Son of man came not to be served but to serve" (Matt. 20:28) ; as the leader of commendable enterprises in the community, he remembers how Jesus "went about doing good" (Acts 10:38) ; and as a preacher, there is always the dependable "Woe to me if I do not preach the gospel!" (1 Cor. 9:16.) For his moments of depression these words come with quiet strength, and when he is face to face with some particularly difficult problem that seems to challenge his very validity and to suggest compromise or even resignation, he says to himself again, "Woe to me if I do not preach the gospel!" He then knows how impossible it is for him to find happiness anywhere else.

The real value of these words, however, comes to him by experience. It would be well if another word came to him by way of a friend—early in his ministry, perhaps even before he began to consider it seriously as a lifework. That word is "Woe to me if I do preach!" It is sensible to consider what will happen to one's life if he does not follow a given way; but it is just as sensible to consider what will happen if he does.

Five times I have received at the hands of the Jews the forty lashes less one. Three times I have been beaten with rods; once I was stoned. Three times I have been shipwrecked; a night and a day I have been adrift at sea; on frequent journeys, in danger from rivers, danger from robbers, danger from my own people, danger from Gentiles, danger in the city, danger in the wilderness, danger at sea, danger from false brethren; in toil and hardship, through many a sleepless night, in hunger and thirst, often without food, in cold and exposure. And, apart from other things, there is the daily pressure upon me of my anxiety for all the churches. (II Cor. 11:24-28.)

There is the staggering catalogue of experiences that were Paul's because he did preach the gospel. How properly some friend might have said to him at Damascus, "Woe to you if you do preach." From that list flash words that are written upon the heart of every minister: "danger from my own people . . . danger from false brethren . . . through many a sleepless night . . . the daily pressure upon me of my anxiety for all the churches." It is no wonder that so many yield to at least a temporary despair; the real wonder is that so few are conquered by it. The reason that they are not is the reason for all ministering: "I am not alone, for the Father is with me." (John 16:32.)

The way of the minister is not always a clearly defined one. It cannot be said that it always "stands forth in sunny outline, brave and clear." The poet Longfellow may find a satisfying analogy in the reflection of the moonlight on the sea—"the whole sea was flashing with this heavenly light, though we saw it only in a single track"; but there are times when the moon is not even visible. Then, indeed, we need to look upon life with "that inward eye which is the bliss of solitude."

It is to such experiences of preaching that we direct our attention and thought. The resolution of our confusions comes not from some new and startling discovery, but from some quiet journeyings back to the place from whence we came, there to see again the face of the One who sent us forth.

ROBERT E. KEIGHTON

Contents

Chapter I

Confusions Come Early

The congregation sings Amen; the last notes of the organ quietly die away. There is a settling of the congregation into the mood and manner of an audience. The minister stands quietly behind the pulpit, waiting for the excitement within him to subside so that his voice may have only the calm compulsion of the pastor. The moment has come; he is to preach his first sermon to the people of his first church. For these are his pepole now, as he is now their pastor.

This is the moment for which he has spent years of preparation and to which his thought and dreams have led his imagination. It is truly a great hour! Others will come, but this is supreme and never-to-be-forgotten. If this moment of transfiguration could only be prolonged and tabernacles be built, wherein he might continue in this mood of exaltation! But it is not to be so. There will be other mountains—some of prayer, some of temptation, and some of compassion for the bewildered and the injured. There will also be valleys of service to the needy, plains of simple teaching, gardens of agony, and perhaps even one hill higher than any mountain. What then? Will he remember this mountain of transfiguration? And if he does, will it explain and compensate for his lesser moments? Or will it only make their shadows the deeper in the light of a setting sun?

The preacher has inevitable moments of despair, frustration, and defeat. It cannot be otherwise. He does not live a secluded existence, nor does he merely accept life; he challenges it and seeks to make it nobler, and these very ambitions lead him over difficult paths. Consider just a few of these. He is to be a truthful and helpful interpreter of the Bible; he is to preach sermons commendable by many standards of judgment; he is to make religion real and God available; he is to provide the influence, the motive, and the power for the highest and best life in man. He must maintain his personal character and integrity, and like Caesar's wife, be utterly above suspicion. Such tasks assume the proportion of the labors of Hercules.

In the consideration of his tasks the minister first sits down with himself, for he knows that no one speaks better than he is. If he attempts it, the devastating plague of insincerity covers the face he shows to his hearers. In order to preach better he must be better. To submit oneself to the scrutiny of life is to discover the need for careful discrimination between seemingly identical twins of experience. Many have believed they were exercising caution when they were really being cowardly; or have called their action tolerance when patronage would have been more truthful. So the preacher must first resolve the confusion of similar experiences.

A friend of mine constantly misuses the words "uninterested" and "disinterested." He is likely to call a judge uninterested and a sleeping member of his congregation disinterested. So must a preacher distinguish between his

14

being dissatisfied and his being unsatisfied. There are times when he feels unusually low in spirit and wonders if the ministry has any real contributions to make to his satisfaction—if it was after all a wrong choice for his life's vocation. Was he really "called"? Perhaps what he thought was a heavenly vision and a voice from the clouds was actually an auditory and visual mirage, or even spots before his spiritual eyes and a ringing in his spiritual ears, as the result of some temporary emotional indigestion. He must, at a time like this, determine whether he is dissatisfied or merely unsatisfied. Is he "cabin'd, cribb'd, confined, bound in to saucy doubts and fears" by the distastefulness and inadequacies of his task; or has he need of knowing that "a man's reach should exceed his grasp"? The restlessness may be the stirrings of greater hopes and promises, the call to leave an inadequate Ur and to go out not knowing whither he goeth. To be dissatisfied is to be beaten; to be unsatisfied is to be inspired.

The artist unsatisfied with his painting and the poet striving for better words to express his thoughts are not dissatisfied with art and literature. They are in the grip of a longing for a better expressive skill, a vocabulary adequate for the demands of an experience. The feeling of never in all one's life having done complete justice to the requirements of an ideal or an inspiration is a feeling that is denied to the immature and the hasty. It is not Thoreau replying to a question about what was his favorite dish with "The nearest one," but Tennyson writing of one who "stands on the heights of his life with a glimpse of a height that is higher." A minister must be critically aware of the difference between the feeling of dissatisfaction at the close of an inadequately preached sermon of skimped preparation, and the yearning of unsatisfied desire that comes only when what he tried to do was so great and so compellingly important that he could not do it well. A man must learn to preach the things that lay hold upon him rather than the things that he has laid hold upon. He can possess the latter, but he can lose them, too.

In *Pilgrim's Inn* Elizabeth Goudge has David ask the clergyman Hilary, "Don't you lose heart? Wonder what's the good of it all in this world where whatever you do it's no use?" To which Hilary makes reply:

Only when I have bronchitis. . . . The superior strength of evil is a numerical superiority, not one of quality. Outside time, numbers have no meaning—only quality. . . . This sense of futility. . . . It's nothing, merely the reverse side of aspiration, and inevitable, just as failure is inevitable. Disregard them both. What can we expect when we aspire as we do, yet remain what we are?

When we have learned to distinguish, convincingly and helpfully, between these two moods of dissatisfaction and unsatisfaction, we shall also have learned the secret of their corollary moods: satisfaction and contentment. Curiously, the answer to either dissatisfaction or unsatisfaction is not satisfaction, but contentment. Satisfaction is a cousin to satiety, and satiety is fullness and consequent lethargy, even boredom. Contentment, on the other hand, is the state of being contained. The translators of the King James Version have Paul say: "I have learned in whatsoever state I am, therewith to be content," (Phil. 4:11)—a translation of the word *autarkes* with which subsequent translators have been satisfied. Properly so, for *autarkes* means self-contained, self-sufficient, having within oneself the power to meet a situation adequately.

Perhaps the restlessness so frequently found in the ministry is most often one of dissatisfaction, but occasionally it is an unrecognized challenge. While many are disappointed in their ministry, some are suffering the keen awareness of incompleteness. The cures are different; discover first the illness.

In the last year of his life Beethoven was found by a friend talking to himself. "Poor Beethoven," said the great composer, "there is no happiness for you in this world; only in the realms of the ideal will you find strength to conquer yourself." Schumann and his wife, Clara, kept a joint diary. After he had presented his Symphony Number 4 to her as a birthday gift, he wrote: "One thing makes me happy—the consciousness of being still far from my goal and obliged to keep doing better, and then the feeling that I have strength to reach it." [1]

That is why when a minister says, "I preached a good sermon yesterday," there is good reason to be suspicious—not of the sermon but of the preacher. We are not to preach good sermons, but to influence lives. To say that we have preached a good sermon may be only to express a certain sense of relief at having met a situation without a feeling of too great frustration; or it may be merely the recognition that this particular experience was better than others less pleasant. If the statement is little more than thinking aloud,

[1] *The Music Lover's Handbook*, ed. Elsie Siegmeister. (New York: William Morrow and Co., 1943), pp. 417, 461.

it can be understood and appreciated. If it be a serious judgment, there is much to be said.

First, we ought to say that the usual conception of "writing a sermon or preaching a sermon" is a faulty approach to our task. It leaves us feeling that the most important work has been done when we have typed the last word, bundled up the pages and put them away for future use. What we have done thus far is not the sermon at all; the sermon is what takes place in the church on Sunday. It is a man talking to a congregation in an intimate exchange of spirit. Until we have come to terms with this conception, we may write the finest set of words ever penned, and still be poor preachers.

The student asks, "What is the best way to prepare a sermon? Should I write it out fully? Do I preach from an outline or from memory, or do I read what I have written?" If these questions are answered from the point of view from which they are asked, there can result only a method of speaking what one has prepared to speak. The real question should begin with a consideration of how a man speaks in public. How does he feel when he faces an audience; does his mind operate easily or awkwardly when he preaches to his congregation? After answering these questions in his own mind, he may then proceed to ask, "What is the best way to *prepare myself* to say what I want to say?" Then the writing of a sermon is seen in its proper relation.

The students of radio have put the situation neatly. They say that a radio program is not the script, nor the performance in the studio, nor even what goes out over the air. The radio program is what takes place in the being of the listener. Therefore, a program is written, directed, acted, and broadcast with one objective in mind—the effect it will have upon the individuals who hear it. A change of phrasing, the introduction of sound effects, the elimination of a character, are not thought of as making a better program, but as achieving a better result in the listener.

We preachers should remember this. Our sermon is not the written notes nor the full manuscript; nor is preaching essentially what we say and do in the pulpit. The sermon is what takes place in the lives of our hearers, and preaching is influencing human lives.

When we write, we pay attention to the rules of grammar. We soon learn, however, that grammar is not the end of good writing, but only its beginning. There follow rhetoric, poetry, and all the forms and styles of writing that go beyond mere correctness. We begin to write well when we learn that writing correctly is only the first step. The plodding efforts of a student still wrestling with the rules of grammar never produced great literature. The concern of a preacher as to whether he has written a good sermon is often merely a sign of immaturity. The boast that he has written a good sermon is under the suspicion that he has not yet learned what such a sermon really is. Many a man has felt pleased with himself after a service of preaching—but notice the phrase "with himself." He is probably moved by the conviction that he has said what he wanted to say and said it correctly and logically; and that he has fulfilled his part of the bargain and now is willing to leave to others the fulfillment of their part. But one cannot remove himself so completely from the final result of preaching. Great preachers have not been those who preached great sermons; they have been those who have influenced their hearers and changed their lives.

The only man who is satisfied with his sermons is the one who has a low standard of preaching. All great preaching must give a sense of futility to the one who preaches. We struggle with an idea, a feeling, a truth that is too big for us; we strive for an objective that recedes like the horizon. These things remain ever beyond us; we cannot lay hold upon them, but only be laid hold of by them. They are not wholly things we possess, but things that possess us. It has been said of the Rich Young Ruler that he had great possessions, but that nothing really great possessed him. When that is said of the preacher, he, too, must turn away sorrowing.

How can we put into words the things that matter most, and if we try—as we are pledged to do—how can we do it adequately? When we have fully satisfied ourselves that we have completely stated in words what we feel, then we have admitted that we are slaves to words and not to feelings, ideas, or truths; we have confessed that what we have captured by words is perhaps nothing more than words themselves. If we can completely put into words what is in our souls, then we must admit that we have felt and believed nothing greater than words. If God can be explained in words, then he is nothing more than a word. If the word salvation expresses our relation to him, then we can alter that relationship by the mere misspelling of the word. There are some who spell and pronounce the word atonement as "at-one-ment" and feel a sense of keen accomplishment. As well repeat "that blessed word Mesapotamia" until its hypnotic influence produces inertia, and call it peace. If such satisfaction is to be desired in preaching, it is easy to obtain, but is a deceitful reward. Rather let the man examine himself for signs of a divine discontent. Here, purged of the dross of mere weakness and sloth, is the golden nugget that proclaims a deposit of rich ore.

All normal individuals have a sense of inadequacy. It is impossible for us to live up to our highest ideals or to the expectations of others—our friends and our families. We doubt our ability to achieve self-imposed demands, to attain the requirements of our position, and to obey the laws of God. This is normal; but it is abnormal for these ideas to become patternized into complexes of loneliness, fear, and defeat. A normal man will maintain a nice balance of distinction between the depression of disappointment and the challenge of incompleteness. Thus, the thirty-eight-year-old Emerson wrote in his Journal for April 6, 1842: "I am *Defeated* all the time; yet to Victory I am born." Remember that ambition is not satisfied by success as hunger is by food. Alexander sighed for more worlds to conquer; victories achieved are goals devaluated.

In *The Heart of the Matter* Graham Greene tells the story of a man enmeshed in the conflicts of life. He is so beset with disaster that he feels that his very presence brings unhappiness to all who know him. He lives in a state of growing and consuming despair. Nevertheless he makes his decisions and is fully prepared to accept the responsibility for his actions—no matter how far that may carry him and others. Greene writes of this situation:

Despair is the price one pays for setting oneself an impossible aim. It is, one is told, the unforgivable sin, but it is a sin that

21

the corrupt or evil man never practises. He always has hope. He never reaches the freezing point of knowing absolute failure. Only the man of good will carries always in his heart this capacity for damnation.[2]

Here is a new kind of damnation and it seems strange that it should be the mark of a man of good will. How startling is the concept that makes it even desirable. Perhaps, then, the minister should search his soul for some evidence of a wholesome despair—one growing out of his high ideals and one that marks the area where he fights what must always be a losing battle. A losing battle it is; for, if he win, he must have been fighting the wrong enemy. This is the divine discontent.

Another confusion is also a cause of unrest. When the writer was in the first year of his ministry, he circulated among his church and community his version of "The Ten Commandments of a Church Member." A friend, upon receiving a copy, wrote him a letter that contained this unforgettable sentence: "This is the way to notoriety, not to fame." How many have confused these two—notoriety and noteworthiness. They look so much alike when they are young, so different when they mature.

A minister wishes to be well known, as he wishes to be well liked. More than most men he has the opportunity to be before people. His very position in a community makes him a public figure. Invitations are numerous to speak before groups of men and women, to appear at the school and the college, to join the lodge or the club, to be a trustee of the library or hospital, or a member of some civic

[2] (New York: The Viking Press, 1948), p. 61.

committee. Some men in the ministry have held high political office. Where the minister cannot go personally, his words may speak for him as they appear in books, magazines, and papers. It is easy for him to be well known. In fact it is more difficult than he often fondly thinks for him not to be.

And what does he achieve by all this—notoriety or noteworthiness? They are easily confused. Any act he does or word he speaks may lead to either; so that the "what" is not easily answered. It lies, rather, with the "how" and the "why." It is startling to realize that not even service in the public interest is necessarily free from the possible taint of notoriety. "Charity shall cover the multitude of sins" in a way not often suspected—but not for long, and never for the sinner.

There is something very subtle in the whole matter; for, is there not value in being well known? If the minister is little known, who will come to hear him; and if few come to hear him, what great good can he do? It is not unreasonable to assume that by his becoming well known through his preaching, he establishes relationships with people that they recall and use when desiring personal counseling and advice. Does this mean, then, that there is a sequence of cause and effect between popularity and success? What treacherous words we have now begun to use! Even if there be such relationship—which is doubtful —we still have the problem of determining which is cause and which is effect. The best judgment seems to be that neither is the cause of the other. Here let us deny the charge that such a judgment can come only from those disappointed, and hence envious, souls who have missed

popularity. Judgments of those who have what we lack
are not always sour grapes.

Before we go too far in this matter we ought to pause for
a moment to listen to a word of Dean Inge that shows
him, at the age of eighty-eight, still somewhat short of
being optimistic. Yet what he says is a word that may have
some caution for our eagerness to be heard by larger
and still larger congregations. Witness the flocking of
preachers to the microphone! "Preaching," said the Dean
"is like throwing a bucketful of water over a row of narrow-
necked vessels. A drop or two may find its way in here
and there." [3] Although we shall never discredit and thus
abandon the sermon as part of the minister's opportunity,
we probably do need a new evaluation of its effectiveness
and a new study of its limitations.

A third confusion is that between anxiety and concern.
Let us approach the problem by recalling a phrase that oc-
curs five times in the sixth chapter of the Gospel According
to Matthew. The King James Version has it as "taking
thought." The translators of this version have made ob-
scure for twentieth-century readers what was perfectly
clear to the Elizabethans. Why should we "take no thought
of tomorrow"? Would that not be foolish and lead to an
improvident tomorrow? Of course it would! The phrase
is properly translated in modern versions as "be not
anxious." This is a different matter. We are not to show
anxiety about food, drink, and clothes—and especially
about tomorrow. Anxiety is a form of irreligion; when we
are worried about tomorrow we are doubtful about God.
Doubt and fear are forms of atheism.

[3] Quoted from AP report in the *Philadelphia Inquirer,* July 29, 1948.

Concern is quite different. The Friends know what it means when they say "we have a concern." It is a deep, moving concentration of attention upon something that stirs the mind and heart. Anxiety leaves us frustrated and sends our senses in a scattered succession of weak efforts. Concern gathers our powers and concentrates our energies upon a focal point of interest and need. Anxiety does something to us; concern makes us do something for others. Anxiety is selfish and turns its gaze inward upon the self; concern is centrifugal and looks out upon the lives of others.

The anxious minister is a liability to himself and to his people. The minister who is truly concerned about life is a commanding general not only of his own forces, but also of those about him. The history of the Church is replete with the lives of those we call "great," but such greatness is always the designation of men and women who have been concerned for the welfare of others. They followed some gleam; some bit of knowledge or some light. What did it matter that there were times when the gleam "waned to a wintry glimmer on icy fallow and faded forest"; that "our knowledge is a torch of smoky pine that lights the pathway but one step ahead";[4] that there were times when the light seemed to be "the light that never was, on sea or land?"

Our greatest need in the ministry today would often seem to be concerns as great as those that motivated and empowered those who came before us. We may call them old-fashioned in their concerns, and very likely we have repudiated the validity of the claims laid upon them by

[4] George Santayana, "O World."

their concern, but we have sinned grievously by failing to espouse a similarly great cause. We have forgotten the story of a demon, an empty house, a householder who only cleaned and did not replace, and the consequent multiple inhabitation that made the latter portion of that house worse than the former. It seems to be a sin today to be greatly concerned about anything. History is a correcting perspective; science is our Aladdin's lamp; psychiatry is a marvelous combination of divining rod and philosophers' stone; and even God has become an affectionate grand-father or—at least—an understanding uncle.

Under those conditions it would seem to be rather silly for us to pray by the hour for the soul of a friend, or to spend time lying awake at night in anguish for the welfare of a son or daughter. Perhaps it is rather silly, but until we can demonstrate that Indifference is God and Micawber is his prophet, we may still do well to cry "Abba, Father." Ministers have developed great skill in allaying the ab-normal fears and complexes of others; now let them turn some attention to the development of healthful concerns of their own.

Of still another confusion the words of Oscar Wilde will suffice. In *Lady Windermere's Fan* Cecil Graham asks, "What is a cynic?" The aphoristic reply of Lord Darling-ton is, "A man who knows the price of everything, and the value of nothing." Wilde must have liked that idea, be-cause he had also said it in *The Picture of Dorian Gray* two years before.

To this may be added merely the observation that the minister needs to know both the cost and the value of all things, but frequently a greater knowledge is the cost of refusal or denial. Paul did say, "Woe to me, *if I do not preach the gospel!*"

Finally, the minister must understand the difference between reputation and character. Reputation is what others say about us and character is what we really are: but, do not stop with anything that easy. The description admits three possibilities: we are better than others think we are; we are worse than they think; what they say and what we are, agree. The first group is the majority; the second group is the hypocrites; the last are either saints or devils. Is there any question about a minister's choice? It is not conceivable that he can long be the pastor of a people if his character undercuts his reputation. He cannot be effective if he must constantly solace his injuries by secret recourse to a private conviction that his character overrides whatever reputation he may have. There is peace and influence only when he and his shadow are identical.

In all these confusions there is a position to be taken that insures stability. There is a principle he may evoke to guide him. A point of view is necessary. Where does he stand with relation to his confusions; what will give him spiritual resources?

Is it true that much of our preaching is concerned with unimportant things? Are we playing about with ephemera? As we go in for light and escapist reading, do we also preach sermons that will do no harm to anyone and may do some good to someone?

> And we are here as on a darkling plain
> Swept with confused alarms of struggle and flight,
> Where ignorant armies clash by night.[5]

[5] Matthew Arnold, "Dover Beach."

That, too often, is the impression we give to others and—God forgive us—too often also the secret conviction we have of the nature of our own efforts. What we need is the word of Oliver Wendell Holmes. It is his challenge to our orientation.

"It isn't where a pawn stands on the board that makes the difference, but what the game round it is, when it is on this or that square." So, the colloquial "What goes on around here?" may be the pass key to the secret treasure of preaching.

We have examined certain confusions that come to the preacher and have suggested some considerations for their resolution. There is no minimizing the perils that lie in wait for us; it is a dangerous thing to become a preacher. Should any man risk it?

In John Masefield's *Coming of Christ* there is a long discussion of what it means for the Spirit of Christ to become Jesus. The Power, The Sword, The Mercy, and The Light all try to dissuade Anima Christi from becoming a man. They point out all the dangers, the hardships, and the defeats. Finally they ask, "Were it not wiser not to enter Life?" The reply of Anima Christi is:

> So be it, then.
> But, the attempt, being worthy, should be made.
> Having beheld man's misery, sin and death,
> Not to go on were treason.[6]

---

[6] Used by permission of the publishers, The Macmillan Co.

Chapter II

Comparisons May Be Dangerous

To the frustrations of confusion must be added—for separate and single consideration—the frustrations of comparison. Probably the most familiar malapropism is one that antedates that famous archetype of linguistic confusion. It is not Mrs. Malaprop, but Dogberry who tells us that "Comparisons are odorous." [1] But Dogberry's creator has given another of his creations a more literary revelation of the canker of comparison. Iago contemplates favorably the killing of Cassio because—says he—"He hath a daily beauty in his life that makes me ugly." [2] Comparison is inevitable, and properly done is invaluable. To avoid it becoming a frustration is our present consideration.

We cannot seem to avoid making comparisons, either with ourselves or with others, whether these latter are better or worse than ourselves. Do you remember the old way—is it only an old way—by which our parents had us measure our height with that of the boy or girl next door? They had us stand back to back and then anounced, "Why you are taller than I thought!" We still measure ourselves thus, standing back to back, or perhaps now face to face, and so discover how much taller or shorter we are than

[1] William Shakespeare, "Much Ado About Nothing," Act III, scene 5.
[2] William Shakespeare, "Othello," Act V, scene 1.

29

our neighbor. Before we go too far we should recall the word of Keats:

> Half-happy, by comparison of bliss,
> Is miserable.[3]

And so it is. But it is difficult to know whether this comparison is a matter of making us miserable because we see the bliss of which we have only a half-portion, and so become unhappy whereas previously we were properly happy. Instead it may be that we are miserable once we see that what we have thought was perfection or joy, is really only our unenlightened judgment that needs a higher goal and a better standard to make us uncomfortably aware that we have not yet come to perfection. This is a genuine reason for being miserable instead of complacent.

What about this comparison with others; is it in terms of quantity or of quality? Do we notice how much more our friends have or how much better they are? This is not a distinction without a difference—quite the opposite. Much of our comparison is in one of these two manners. We are like the awed disciples when they saw the Temple. But is our comment in the translation of Moffatt or the Revised Standard Version? Moffatt gives us the remark of the disciples as, "Look, teacher, what a size these stones and buildings are!" (Mark 13:1). The R.S.V. has, "Look, Teacher, what wonderful stones and what wonderful buildings!" It does seem to make a difference which way we translate our comparisons with others.

Sometimes we recognize that our friends have the same qualities that we have, but they possess them in greater

[3] "Endymion," Bk. II.

abundance. How awkward it is to travel with a companion who has a great deal more money than we have. But it is no less awkward to travel with one who has a greater appreciation of what he sees! In both instances we are embarrassed, if not humiliated. We find that we cannot always go to the same places, and even when we do there is a likelihood that we shall not do the same things or enjoy the same pleasures. Certainly our appreciation of values will differ from that of our companion. Soon we begin to resent the differences and then envy has a clear course. Thus we have traveled the course that began with a mere recognition of the differences in quantity, proceeded to an awareness that there were also differences in quality, and ended in a state of envy of the person himself. How quickly we transfer from the impersonal to the personal; we begin with "what" and we end with "who." Abstract ideas do not long remain independent entities; like parasites they require living beings to remain alive.

What is it, then, that we envy in others? Is it their talents, their abundance, their use of what they have, their skills, or their successes? We would do well to begin by knowing exactly what it is that we are comparing, and to give considerable attention to the focal center of our frustration. We do better to recognize that our envy of others, from whatever cause or of whatever possession, is a wasteful emotion and an expensive privilege. No one can afford envy.

Let us not, however, get too far away from the comparison with ourselves. How often have we felt less happy here! We know that we are not what we might or could be; we do not write that book, paint that picture, or even repair that piece of furniture down in the cellar. Some day we will get around to it, but today isn't the day. It becomes difficult to know whether the trouble is inability or just plain procrastination. Wasn't there a saint who prayed, "Make me better, Lord, but not just now"? The strangest part of our self-comparison is that we very rarely find ourselves without an excuse—which we dignify by calling it a reason—for being what we are and not what we feel we could be. Have you noticed how we judge ourselves in a game of golf? Our drive goes all of fifty yards, our second shot slices off to the next fairway, and when we are on in eight and take three putts of four feet each, we say (provided of course that at this point we are capable of articulate speech), "I am certainly off my game today!" What superb optimism and confidence! One straight, long drive or one twenty-foot putt and "Now, I'm really playing my game!" Self-comparisons are not always too trustworthy.

The ancients were right when they said, "Know thyself," and Plutarch was also right when he remarked: "If it were a thing obvious and easy for every man to *know himself,* the precept had not passed for an oracle." It is exceedingly hard for a man to know himself; especially to know his changing self which seems not to be the same today that it was yesterday and will be different tomorrow. We are too many selves and seem to be fighting a civil war within at any moment. Yet it does not seem too much to say that we must come to some intelligent and workable understanding of precisely what we are and what to expect of ourselves before we can know whether to blame our self or our selves. Somewhere there is help for a foundation of judgment. Robert Frost's lines about an axe handle are in point. He writes,

> The lines of a good helve
> Were native to the grain before the knife
> Expressed them, and its curves were no false curves
> Put on it from without. And there its strength lay
> For the hard work.[4]

It would save us a lot of quite unnecessary and unprofitable worry if we were to remember that truth. Too often we have been besieged by the injunction to make more of ourselves, until we have become unwilling to admit that there is a limit to what we can do. It is true, theoretically at least, that every boy in the United States may grow up to be President; what we usually forget is that in any one period of four years only one of those grown-up boys can be President. There can be a lot of nonsense about equality; the word needs most careful and intelligent definition. There are just some things that each of us can never be or do. A dog can hear sounds I can never hear— as my supersonic whistle tells me every time I call him— but does that distress me? It does if I discover that I am really tone-deaf, especially if I have set my heart on being an opera singer. To succeed in the Metropolitan requires more than the mere desire to do so, even when combined with the most arduous and otherwise satisfactory practice and discipline. There is first that small matter of having the native vocal equipment. Thus, if I am color-blind, there is little chance of my becoming a great painter, although there are times when I have seriously considered

[4] "The Axe-Helve," from "New Hampshire": copyright 1923 by Henry Holt & Co., Inc., copyright 1951 by Robert Frost. Used by permission of the publishers.

this as the explanation of some pictures I have seen. If these examples seem farfetched and so very obvious, that is precisely what I want them to be. Other obstacles are just as obvious if we sensibly consider our native limitations.

Thoreau wrote, "Pursue, keep up with, circle round and round your life, as a dog his master's chaise. Do what you love. Know your own bone; gnaw at it, bury it, unearth it, and gnaw it still." Exactly so: "Know your own bone." (The remainder of this portion of his letter should be read by ministers, but with some caution. It is the first of many letters to Harrison Blake and is dated March 27, 1848.) This word of Thoreau would delight a friend of mine who is constantly reminding me that "a man cannot be what he is not," by which he means no repudiation of possible progress in life. He means—and I agree with him—that we are distinct individuals, and the sooner we learn the exact kind of individual we are, the sooner we stop trying to be what we cannot become, and give our mind and effort to becoming what we are. Let the minister and the preacher note this especially; imitation may be the sincerest form of flattery, although the imitation may be far from flattering to either individual. One of the greatest words of the great Samuel Johnson was, "Almost all absurdity of conduct arises from the imitation of those whom we can not resemble."

The confusion that results when we discover that we do not make a favorable object of comparison either with another or with our own self, may actually be the result of the basic discovery that we are not really either omniscient or omnipotent. This comes as a strange truth to some, who resemble Tom Towers. "It is probable that Tom Towers," writes Trollope in *The Warden,* "considered himself the most powerful man in Europe; and so he walked on from day to day, studiously striving to look a man, but knowing within his breast that he was a god." Indeed, that must be a hard pose to hold, maintaining a balance between one's prestige and one's vanity.

Why should we have to say that no one of us knows everything and that no one of us can do everything? Perhaps because so many of us think we do and can. Sometimes it does seem as though preachers were especially culpable. A friend of mine was telling me that he was going to preach on a question asked him by a schoolboy. "Say, Doc," asked the lad, "what's life amount to, anyway?" Said my friend, "I'm going to answer that question." Perhaps it was my real friendship with Doc that allowed me to answer as I did with, "If you ever want a sure means of overcoming that temptation, read the section on 'Life' in Stevenson's *Home Book of Quotations.* That has cured me many times." (For those who do not have Stevenson handy, let us here record that the section is divided into thirty heads, and covers almost forty pages. That acts as a slight deterrent to saying with any assurance whatever, "Life is . . .") Then I added, "But I suppose if we knew how much had been preached about anything we essay, we wouldn't preach it." But, again, the attempt being worthy and desperately needed, must be made. We cannot avoid the danger of being inadequate by choosing to be inarticulate. Besides, it is rarely necessary to answer the whole question or to solve the entire problem; generally it is only a small portion of it that requires our attention.

We should learn very early to leave the involved metaphysics to the metaphysicians; and become practical physicians ourselves, even though we shall have to answer the charge, "Physician, heal thyself."

At this point let us see that our best procedure may be not to answer the question at all, but to answer the questioner. We are not solving a problem, but an individual's problem; we are not giving answers, but help. It is a wise minister who tells his wife not to interrupt him after she has heard him give an answer to Mr. Jones that is diametrically opposite to the answer he gave Mr. Smith who asked the same question yesterday. There is no necessary reason why the same answer should be given to two different people, even on the same day. Mr. Jones and Mr. Smith are two different persons; and even Mr. Jones is a different person today than he was yesterday or will be tomorrow. The same question asked by two men, or by the same man on two different occasions, may not be the same question. Jesus himself is our reference for this fact. In Luke 10:25 ff. a lawyer asked him, "Teacher, what shall I do to inherit eternal life?" Jesus probed by asking him, "What is written in the law? How do you read?"; and the lawyer's reply led to the parable of the Good Samaritan. In Luke 18:18 a ruler asked him, "Good Teacher, what shall I do to inherit eternal life?"; Jesus first asked him, "Why do you call me good? . . . You know the commandments." The man answered, "All these have I observed from my youth," which elicited from Jesus, "Sell all that you have and distribute to the poor. . . ." It is not hard to see that these two answers to the same question are so because the men who asked the question were different men with different reasons for asking the question, and consequently needed different ways of seeing their own positions with relation to the question. So, it is well to answer the person rather than the question.

We have said that no one can know everything or do everything. This is certainly an axiom. The trouble comes when we think otherwise. Many times I recall a word of my father, and none more often than his "You don't know how much you have to know in order to know how little you know." His was, of course, a free adaptation of the words of many of the ancients—words we have neglected to our hurt. Perhaps it is not so much that we have neglected them, as that we have feared them and the consequences to our reputation if we took them seriously. One of the rarest answers in the world is a sincere and humble, "I do not know." It is rarely to be found either in the pulpit or the classroom. Listen then, to Abraham Flexner: "We have become increasingly and painfully aware of our abysmal ignorance. No scientist, fifty years ago, could have realized that he was as ignorant as all first-rate scientists now know themselves to be." [5] For "scientists" substitute "preacher," and see if you are satisfied.

It is no place of refuge to hide behind the statement that we cannot answer even the easiest questions. How then can we answer the hard ones? What are easy questions? There is properly no such thing as an easy question; and an easy answer is suspect of shallowness in understanding the question. It is also probably deceitful. I was absolutely convinced that I was an educated young man when I graduated from college, that I was prepared for the

[5] *Universities* (New York: Oxford University Press, 1930), pp. 17-18.

ministry when I graduated from the seminary. Today, I am even more convinced that I shall never again know as much as I did on either of those occasions.

On this matter of the easy answer Van Wyck Brooks has something to say that should be given serious consideration. It may be found in his *Opinions of Oliver Allston:*

> A young man is writing a book on the future of society. What steps should we take to make the world better? He wants a few lines from "thinkers of the older generation." Would I send him a paragraph about it? . . .
>
> But what interests me is this holding people up for their opinions, asking them what they think at the point of a pistol. . . . What are these opinions worth . . . ? They cannot come from the depths of the mind. They can only come from the mental pockets in which we carry our small change. . . . I do not propose to hand out unripe fruit, and I deplore these bunches of green bananas.[6]

There is another facet of this confusion that arises from the sense of our inability to achieve on a level with our desires. We are disturbed by the knowledge that there are so many needs in our congregations, so many varying questions being mutely asked us. How can we possibly meet such demands? Here is the true frustration of inadequacy. But is frustration necessary? Hardly—if we have seen our inadequacy in the true light, it will cast its shadows only in the proper places. We can begin by seeing that if we have not the absolute answer, the ready solution, we may have the confidence that there is an answer and a solution, and that they can and may become known. This is, indeed,

[6] (New York: E. P. Dutton & Co., Inc., 1941), pp. 44-45. Used by permission.

the faith of the scientist who labors for a solution he believes will come to him in due time. It is believing that there is a cure for cancer that prompts all our research as well as the financial support of such research. We do not yet have the answer, but tomorrow is another day. What stimulates and strengthens us is the fact that this very tomorrow may falsify our last statement. If we have this same hope and faith in our preaching, we shall have done much to see that where we cannot answer the question, we have nevertheless answered the questioner.

Our congregations are a varied group and they bring to us a wide area of interests and needs. To compare our equipment with their demands may bring more than uneasiness. Especially is this true if we demand of ourselves that we say something new about their problems. (We shall have something to say about originality in a later chapter. Here let us address ourselves to another side of this matter.) Somerset Maugham in *The Summing Up* has told us that it is unlikely that a dramatist will have the good fortune to possess both something remarkable to say and the remarkable ability to say it well. He says:

How can you write a play of which the ideas are so significant that they will make the critic of *The Times* sit up in his stall and at the same time induce the shop-girl in the gallery to forget the young man who is holding her hand? . . . It is not any sort of dramatist who can find anything to say about them that has not been said a thousand times already; the great truths are too important to be new.

Let us say that again. "The great truths are too important

to be new." We shall need to return to that statement often.

One of the questions we hear asked over and over again is: "Do we have to have experience of the things we preach?" That question has many forms and ways of being asked. Can we preach about anything unless we have had an experience of it? Will anyone heed us if we talk about something they know more about than we do, and how can we be sure that in any given instance they do not know much more than we do? How can we young men preach to older folks? These are some of the perplexing questions raised by men who want to preach, but are deterred by the fear that they have neither the knowledge nor the experience required.

Perhaps there is something in what Trollope says in *Barchester Towers:*

> It often surprises us that very young men can muster courage to preach for the first time to a strange congregation. Men who are as yet but little more than boys, who have but just left, what indeed we may not call a school, but a seminary intended for their tuition as scholars, . . . ascend a rostrum high above the heads of the submissive crowd, not that they may read God's word to those below, but that they may preach their own word for the edification of their hearers. It seems strange to us that they are not stricken dumb by the new and awful solemnity of their position. . . . Has my newly acquired privilege, as one of God's ministers, imparted to me as yet any fitness for the wonderful work of a preacher?

How can a young man preach to older folks; indeed, how can he preach at all? To ask that question is to look at only one side of the problem, and to ask only one question about preaching. The sober and alarming truth is not that it is hard for a young man to preach under these conditions, but that it is hard for anyone to preach under any conditions. It is harder for an older man to preach than it ever was for the young man; age brings its own kind of fear. Youth knows the fear of the unknown; age the fear of the known. The young man is afraid, but his fear arises from his imagination; the older man is afraid because of what he does know. There is a fear of knowledge as well as a fear of ignorance; and one has not said all the truth when one has remarked, usually too casually, that we are afraid of what we do not know. How simple and helpful that truth would be, if it were the only truth! Many a person has repeated the classic statement that "It is not the parts of the Bible I do not understand that trouble me; it is the parts I understand all too well." Similarly one may well say, "It is not the fear I conjure for myself out of the unknown tomorrow that troubles me, but the fear of what I know exists today."

The older one grows, the harder it is to preach. The easy assurance is gone, and in its place is the haunting memory of mistakes one made because the answer given came too easily. We often name the winner before all the returns are in. Answers we gave at twenty, we should not think of giving at fifty. Many of us say we shall never again know as much as we did when we graduated from the seminary.

All empty souls tend to extreme opinion. It is only in those who have built up a rich world of memories and habits of thought that extreme opinions affront the sense of probability. Propositions, for instance, which set all the truth upon one side can only enter rich minds to dislocate and strain, if they can enter at all, and sooner or later the mind expels them by instinct.[7]

But exactly what is this "experience" we talk about so often? Does it mean doing the things we talk about; having been in the places we describe? If it does, our sermons are going to be severely limited in subjects, as well as in scope. We are driven to the absurd conclusion that we must have ourselves committed the sins we deplore, traveled through Palestine if we are to describe the Crucifixion, and must never express even a belief in immortality. This very *reductio ad absurdum* answers our question. Our sermons contain another kind of experience, to which we must give some attention. It is the kind of experience the young may have as well as the old; age has little to do with it.

Hayakawa has told us about this kind of experience in his *Language in Action*.[8] "Experience itself is an extremely imperfect teacher. Experience does not tell us what we are experiencing. Things simply happen. And if we do not know *what to look for* in our experience, they often have no significance to us whatever." Then he points out that we have a kind of respect for people who, we say, "do things" and "go places." But often such travel and action bring little of the kind of experience we are talking about. "They go to London, and all they remember is their hotel and the American Express Company office; . . . they may be caught in a South American revolution in the course

[7] *The Autobiography of William Butler Yeats* (New York: The Macmillan Co., 1953), pp. 284-85.

[8] (New York: Harcourt, Brace & Co., 1941), pp. 259-60. Used by permission.

of their travels and remember only their personal discomforts." Then Hayakawa makes the astonishing statement that: "The result often is that people who have never had these experiences, people who have never been to those places, know more about them than people who have." Here is the "experience" the preacher may have because he has developed a soul and a mind sensitive to what happens to other people as well as to himself. He has learned how to think as they think, feel as they feel, and to report to others so that they, too, think and feel similarly. The kind of experience the minister must have to preach effectively is the experience that understands and interprets; it is a kind of empathic imagination.

Chapter III

Eternity in an Hour

The minister may preach a sermon about a great final day of judgment, but he faces a day of judgment at the conclusion of every sermon he preaches. What did he say and was it well said? Was it worth saying; was it true? For the moment he becomes a whole courtroom in himself—defendant, prosecutor, jury, and judge. Then later he discovers himself in the one role not his during the case: he becomes an attendant at the session of the court, a spectator at the trial. Then he asks a very impertinent question—what was the whole case about? Was it worth the while of the court; were the ends of justice served?

Indeed, was the whole thing merely a theatrical performance of interest to the spectators, fun for the actors, but of hardly any more lasting value than the concerns of the moment? Here are the crucial question and the final judgment.

The value or pertinency of a single sermon is interesting speculation; the worth of preaching is vital. The doctor may discredit the efficacy of a medicinal treatment, but if he discredit the worth of medicine, per se, he must leave his profession. The minister may discount a sermon, but if he discredit preaching, he is abandoning a procedure.

But do our people really listen to us when we preach? John Donne has a confession that may help us to recognize the frailty that is in the best of us. In a sermon preached at the funeral of Sir William Cokayne, December 12, 1626, he said,

> I throw myself down in my Chamber, and I call in, and invite God, and his Angels thither, and when they are there, I neglect God and his Angels, for the noise of a Fly, for the rattling of a Coach, for the whining of a door; I talk on, in the same posture of praying; Eyes lifted up; knees bowed down; as though I prayed to God; and, if God or his Angels should ask me, when I thought last of God in that prayer, I cannot tell: Sometimes I find that I had forgot what I was about, but when I began to forget it, I cannot tell.

When we are disturbed by the apparent fact that our people remember so little of what we say, it is well for us to make the search a more personal one. Tell me, sir, what did you preach about on Sunday before last? Quickly, now! Perhaps you would have a very difficult time to reproduce now, without recourse to any notes, exactly what you did say. Remembering a sermon is not just what we think it is.

Perhaps, then, the influence of a sermon is not precisely what we believe it to be, and will not be found either by the question we have asked or in the place we have sought to find it. It is more than probable that the influence and the effect of a sermon are far more secure facts precisely because they are so subtle. The gold that lies on the surface is not necessarily the evidence of a vein underneath the ground. And, of course, "all that glitters is not gold."

It ought to be said, however, that this wholesale distrust of preaching is often the Blue Monday mood, a form of infection that is sometimes mild and sometimes virulent. It grows out of the fact that what we wanted did not happen; the change we sought did not come. Perhaps, on a more personal and surely lower level, no one said what we wanted to have said to us and the particular one we wanted to speak to us did not say a word. We are creatures like unto our fellow men, and the mead of praise is an intoxicating draught we desire even as we distrust it.

Yes, this is indeed our Blue Monday mood. No one has described it better than Oliver Wendell Holmes. His Autocrat concludes a comment by asking someone to pass him the pie. As an aside he makes a remarkable confession, that should find a memory and a warning lurking in the minds of most of us who preach!

I took more of it than was good for me—as much as 85°, I should think,—and had an indigestion in consequence. While I was suffering from it, I wrote some sadly desponding poems, and a theological essay which took a very melancholy view of creation. When I got better I labelled them all "Pie-crust," and laid them by as scarecrows and solemn warnings. I have a number of books on my shelves that I should like to label with some such title; but, as they have great names on their title-pages—Doctors of Divinity, some of them—it wouldn't do.

Stopford Brooke, the biographer of Frederick W. Robertson, writes of that famous English preacher that there were passages in his letters indicating his dislike of preaching!

But the passages in which he describes his dislike of preaching and his own coldness of heart are in reality descriptions of the reaction of feeling after the intense excitement of preaching. Such passages are always to be found in letters written on Monday.[1]

It is a personal and human view we take. Talk as much as we will about the long view of life and the eternal patience of God, we ourselves are despairingly myopic and distressingly impatient. The distant city may be worth the arduous journey, but we would like a little pleasant scenery along the way. It is well to believe we are on the right road, but an occasional signpost that confirms our belief is a very welcome sight. If it indicates, also, that we are making progress, we shall not take it amiss.

What is it we expect; what will encourage us? What is a word of approval? Somehow the word "popular" creeps into our awareness, but we are not seekers of popularity; that does not satisfy, it merely pleases. In our better moments, we know that to be popular is to be a child of the populace—ever a precarious and dubious honor. The crowds that cry Hosanna today may still cry crucify tomorrow; they often do. We know that to be so and take such applause easily enough in public, but critically in private. To have our worth assayed by the rough estimate of the carnival weight-guesser is not calculated to make us proud; especially when we recall that in the symbolic art of the Egyptian picture of our judgment before the God, our heart in one balance is being measured in the other by a feather.

[1] *Life and Letters of Frederick W. Robertson* (New York: Harper & Bros., 1867), p. 160.

When anyone decries popularity there are always many who listen to the judgment with minds predisposed to understand it in terms of the speaker's sense of frustration and consequent tang of sour grapes. It is often—perhaps only—the popular who know its real emptiness. If ever a preacher knew and fought against popularity, it was Frederick W. Robertson of Brighton. As a college student he wrote to his mother from Oxford in 1839:

> I hear of M—'s enthusiastic reception at Cheltenham. I do believe the station of a popular preacher is one of the greatest trials on earth. . . . The preacher who causes a great sensation and excited feeling is not *necessarily* the one who will receive the reward of shining as the stars for ever and for ever, because he has turned many to righteousness.[2]

But it was in Brighton that he became the popular "Robertson of Brighton." It is therefore unusually striking to hear him say, "I wish I did not hate preaching so much, but the degradation of being a Brighton preacher is almost intolerable."[3] And on another occasion, perhaps his most picturesque repudiation of popularity: "Would to God I were not a mere pepper-cruet to give relish to the palates of Brightonians!"[4] He wrote: "And how sternly I have kept my tongue from saying a syllable or a sentence, in pulpit or on platform, *because* it would be popular!"[5] He could view his popularity with a kind of objective passion:

> Another Sunday done: crowded congregations, pulpit steps

[2] *Ibid.*, p. 40.
[3] *Ibid.*, p. 259.
[4] *Ibid.*, p. 243.
[5] *Ibid.*, p. 143.

even full, anteroom nearly so. . . . I sat in church thinking, "Now, how this crowd would give many men pleasure, flatter their hearts with vanity, or fill them with honest joy! How strange that it is given to one who cannot enjoy it, who takes no pains to keep it, who would gladly give all up, and feels himself in the midst of all a homeless and heartless stranger!" [6]

That Robertson was popular, no one can doubt. That he was thoroughly suspicious of and antagonistic toward popularity is equally plain. Of course, his view was colored by his personality and aggravated by his growing illness, but this is not the final word about it. Robertson's sincere and often vehement disapproval of any form of his popular approval and acclaim has a ring of genuineness about it that is a tocsin to anyone tempted to think otherwise. Writing about the choice of Ernest Tower to be his curate, he is glad that it will release him for more pastoral work, ". . . at the prospect of which I rejoice; for I can not say how humiliated I feel at degenerating into the popular preacher of a fashionable watering-place." [7] Degenerating into being a popular preacher—that is an idea with which we are not too familiar.

Shall we, on the other hand, be our own judges and measure ourselves for what we have done? Surely there is a serious truth in the statement that if we judge ourselves we have no need of the judgment of others. This worth of self-judgment is a truth that has universal acceptance. Its one fault is its unreliability—indeed its impossibility. We talk of our success as though self-satisfaction were the criterion. But success is in terms of influence

[6] *Ibid.*, p. 180.
[7] *Ibid.*, p. 330.

and ultimate good, and who can measure that? We are critical of those who judge us without knowing our motives. It is just as wrong to judge ourselves if we know only our motives. The returns are not yet all in; we must wait at least until the polls close and the ballots are counted. At best it is a hazardous business—this guessing what one has done well.

One Sunday evening I left my pulpit with a sense of the most utter frustration I had ever known. The sermon had been terrible in its inadequacy, the delivery pitiful in its awkwardness. Every sentence, every word, seemed to have come only after the most appalling struggle. I literally perspired with the effort to be convincing. Floating through my consciousness were the thoughts: "Why did I ever choose this sermon? What did I ever see in it? Will I get through this side of a complete breakdown?" Upon arriving home, I voiced my dismay to an always sympathetic ear, who quite agreed with my judgment. For a brief moment I even considered giving up the ministry. A few weeks later I preached another sermon that I immodestly admitted was the finest ever achieved—it had everything. It should be printed for the universal improvement of mankind.

The next January I circulated the usual ballots for the congregation's vote on those sermons they considered the best of the preceding year and wished to have preached again. The "failure" was voted the best sermon of the year, and the "success" did not receive so much as a single vote. Such is the value of a preacher's judgment about his sermons and his preaching!

There is another way to look at the effectiveness of our

preaching. It is the same way we look at the effectiveness of our living. I shall long remember an experience of my early ministry. A telephone call from a member of the community summoned me urgently to the house of a lady who asked me a most startling question: "You know that part in the marriage service where the minister asks if anyone knows of any reason why the service should not go on? Well, what would you do if someone rose at that point and objected to the marriage?"

My too easy reply, that I never used that part of the service, did not give me the time I needed to formulate an answer, for she pressed the point by asking, "But if you did use it and someone objected, what would you do?"

My only recourse then was to counter with, "Why do you want to know?"

"Because," was the frank and alarming reply, "I am going to do that tomorrow afternoon at my daughter's wedding."

For the next two hours we talked, and then parted with the understanding that she would not do what she had planned. It would have been an ill-conceived retaliation for an unwarranted objection to her future son-in-law. She came to see, also, that apron strings are not dignified by being called silver cords.

Twelve years passed and one afternoon I was standing outside our post office when a woman spoke to me and said, "You don't remember me, do you?" Then she identified herself as the mother who had asked the question, and said: "I have been living in another community for many years and have had no chance of telling you how things turned out. I want you to know that today I am

the happiest grandmother and mother-in-law in the world."
Some acts and some sermons have long fuses!

> Nor knowest thou what argument
> Thy life to thy neighbor's creed has lent.[8]

There is still another way of looking at the effectiveness of our sermons—and that is probably the only valid one. Instead of being concerned with either ourselves or with others, let us examine what we preach, and thus focus our attention upon the message rather than the messenger, important as he may be. There is much to be said for the truth advertised by a drug company that "The priceless ingredient of every product is the honor and integrity of its maker." There is also much to be said for the composition and value of the product itself. One of the judgments against any age has been the triviality of its interests. Perhaps, there is profit in asking about what we preach. The biblical writers called their message the gospel, and the unsearchable riches of Christ. Is ours only "the sermon"?

There is encouragement in the conviction that what we call our work has no ultimate effect upon what it really is. "A rose by any other name" still remains a rose. The permanency or the truth of a statement is independent of the approval or the disapproval of the speaker or the hearer. In this sense my certificate of ordination is quite in error when it boldly states that I have been "set for the defense of the Gospel." It is worth considering that what the world needs is not the defense of the gospel, but the

[8] Ralph Waldo Emerson, "Each and All."

preaching of it; that what man needs most is not the proof that God is, but the evidence of what he is.

Chopin, dying, asked his sister to burn all his unpublished manuscripts. "I owe it to the public and myself, to publish only my best works," he explained. "I have kept to this resolution all my life—I wish to keep to it now." [9]

Suppose ministers were to consider their task as the preaching of their best thoughts rather than the preaching of a sermon each Sunday. Suppose they exchanged the compulsion of having to say something for the impulsion of having something to say. It is a joy to lose the frustrating sense of search and to discover the joy of choice. It is rumored—and widely believed—that the best work comes from inspiration, a word of peculiarly religious connotations. The belief is healthy, but the practice seems to be somewhat sickly.

To return to Robertson just once more. There was a time when he felt preaching to be an intolerable burden. He wrote at Brighton:

The thought of drudging on here at the same work, unvaried; two sermons a Sunday, inspiration by clock-work for several years, is simply the conception of an impossibility. I want perpetually the enthusiasm which comes from fresh views of duty and untrodden paths of usefulness—new impulse from the heart.[10]

His is indeed a worthy desire, but it is an impossible demand. The ideal of perpetual inspiration is high and worthy, and to have one less high is to lower not only one's

[9] Siegmeister, *loc. cit.*, p. 479.
[10] Brooke, *op. cit.*, p. 157.

standard, but one's product as well. But in the real world we all know so well, "inspiration by clock-work," or more properly by calendar, is likely to intrude itself with alarming frequence. The danger is that we shall conclude that it is the necessary alternative to our ideal. This is not so; there are other views we may take of our privilege.

Perhaps the day will come when there will not be a sermon every Sunday, produced only by the inexorability of time. No, I am not going back to that day when we talked glibly about a "moratorium on all preaching." Rather, I am thinking of the time when the minister will announce that he has something to say to his people and will say it a week from Sunday; or, if it cannot wait, he will call a special meeting of the church to hear him on Tuesday evening. There is something haunting about such a prospect. Is there a minister or a church brave enough to make the experiment?

When one takes a view of preaching like that, there is no worry about the permanency of what one says; that is lost in the exciting reward of being a party to creation. Will what I say matter a year from now? Suppose it doesn't —that is little cause for worry if it matter today. I need something of the newspaperman's philosophy expressed by Alexander Woollcott, when he wrote:

I count it a high honor to belong to a trade in which the good man writes each piece, each paragraph, each sentence as lovingly as any Addison, and do so in the full knowledge that by noon the next day it will have been used to light a fire or saved, if at all, to line a shelf.[11]

[11] Samuel Hopkins Adams, *A. Woollcott* (New York: Reynal & Hitchcock, 1947) , p. 147.

This is to say that we do not have to wait for tomorrow to prove eternity; eternity is in the nature of the thing, not in its durability. "He hath set eternity in their heart," is the beautiful word of the American Standard Version's translation of a part of Eccl. 3:11. The quality and the experience of the eternal are not revelations reserved for Heaven. One finds it in a flash of red along a fence rail, in a soft blue patch of sky above the green of the woods, in the poured-out exultation of a thrush; it is seen in the face of a friend and in the silence of a loved one; it is a remembered joy and a hoped-for peace. William Blake was indeed right in his "Auguries of Innocence," which begins:

> To see a world in a grain of sand
> And a heaven in a wild flower,
> Hold Infinity in the palm of your hand
> And Eternity in an hour.

Truly Andrew Fuller spoke for us also when he said, "A pulpit seems an awful place! An opportunity for addressing a company of immortals on their eternal interests; oh how important! We preach for eternity." [12] The pulpit is a place full of awe for the preacher, because he is to be concerned about what is eternal and must ask himself searching questions about his competency and the quality of his preaching. But the pulpit is not a place of despair and preaching is not futile. When James Stewart called his book *Heralds of God,* he was putting the matter in its proper form. In a final sense we are not only ministers

[12] Diary—February 5, 1781.

of a church, pastors of a people, and preachers of sermons, we are heralds of God. Drop "God" out of that sentence, and the first part is reduced to zero.

A ministerial student was examining a paper that he had just taken from his mailbox. It was a term paper that had been returned to him by the professor of theology. The subject assigned had been "The Nature of God." True to his group, the student turned at once to the one thing that was to him of first importance—the last page with the professor's mark for the paper. Looking at it for a moment, Joe turned slowly to the group gathered in the room and said, with his characteristic humorous insight, "I don't see how I'm going to preach with only a C+ God!"

Chapter IV

Even More Than Truth

One of the moot questions, perennially debated, is the relative importance of matter and manner. Which is the more important—what we say or how we say it? To decide in favor of either is fraught with difficulty and latent disaster. If we say that the content is all important and that what we have to say is unquestionably of first consideration, then we are asserting that truth is sufficiently powerful to overcome all handicaps. We quote "Truth, crushed to earth, shall rise again!" So it will. No one believes that it can be destroyed. Conquered or lost in one age, it will appear again—for it is eternal. But our very quotation betrays us. "Crushed to earth"—then it can be overcome and rendered powerless, if only for a moment! Is history not full of instances where men have spoken truth, but to an unheeding world?

On the other hand, if we say that the manner of presentation is more important, we seem to be taking sides with all the charlatans, mountebanks, and madcaps whose stock is mere cleverness and the bizarre. We live in a world where evidence of this abounds—examples are legion. If one simply must have an illustration, let search be made in any book concerned with public speaking that has a chapter on "Gestures." Certainly sanity suggests that what is not worth saying at all is not worth saying well! Therefore, to decide that style is more important than content is to risk the judgment that what we are saying is somehow shallow, trivial, traditional, and worthless. Then perhaps what we are preaching has the value of being only what our fathers thought they had—or what we feel we should have. There can also be vested interests in thoughts.

Henry Ward Beecher once wrote,

> You know how beautifully some men write, and how poorly they deliver; how well they prepare their materials, and yet their materials when prepared are of no force whatever. They are beautiful arrows,—arrows of silver; golden-tipped are they, and winged with the feathers of the very bird of paradise. But there is no bow to draw the arrows to the head and shoot them strongly home, and so they fall out of the sheath down in front of the pulpit or platform.[1]

That preacher is all too familiar. He has thought clearly and studied hard; his words are indeed truth. But when he preaches, his hearers must be patient geniuses in order to be able to follow him, much less be moved by his truths. A Fuller Brush salesman or the announcer for a soap opera has more of doomsday in his voice. We cannot but feel that if the truth means no more to the preacher, it can mean no more to us.

If a good classical text for this is needed, let the need be met by turning to "The Task" by William Cowper. Consult Book II and begin reading at line 395. Read on carefully for about a hundred lines.

[1] "Health, As Related to Preaching," *Yale Lectures*, Series I, lecture 8.

He that negotiates between God and man,
As God's ambassador, the grand concerns
Of judgment and of mercy, should beware
Of lightness in his speech. 'Tis pitiful
To court a grin, when you should woo a soul;
To break a jest, when pity would inspire
Pathetic exhortation; and to address
The skittish fancy with facetious tales,
When sent with God's commission to the heart.

An even fuller discussion and a much longer text is the history of Rhetoric from early Greek times to the present, with a possible emphasis on the Renaissance. Such a text will provide ample material for anyone wishing to discuss the subject—no matter which side of the question he wishes to defend.

There must have been times when Adam considered returning to the garden of Eden. The record does not show that he even tried. Perhaps it was because he always remembered two things: the word of expulsion spoken by God, and the little matter of the Cherubim "and a flaming sword which turned every way" (Gen. 3:24). If Adam wavered at the memory of the word, it is my guess that when remembering the sword, he went right on about his farming.

Thus early in human history what was said was sustained and enforced by the way it was said. Manner and style asserted an early relationship to matter, and have retained that relationship ever since. Moreover, it is not just any relationship; it is a relationship in which matter is supported by manner. In the words of my title, in any act of communication, truth is not enough; even more than truth is the form in which it is communicated. The Bible has it this way: "A word fitly spoken is like apples of gold in a setting of silver" (Prov. 25:11). When manner and matter are suitably combined, the result is a treasure. When they clash, the result is not only unpleasant to the recipient, but disastrous to the truth. Manner can destroy matter!

What this means to those of us who are charged with the privilege of preaching is simply that it is not enough to speak the truth; one must speak it properly. It is not enough to be right; one must be acceptably right. Of course, all this is on the assumption that one wishes to have others accept the truth. If there is no desire even to communicate the truth, then however one offers it is of little consequence to his own relation to it. But we are not merely possessors of truth—such as we have—nor mere believers in that possession. We are committed to sharing our experience of truth, and as such, are charged with the speaking of truth. Just here is our awful responsibility.

We have believed that truth was enough—that it will win its own hearing. We have taken refuge in the delightfully poetic assurance of, "We needs must love the highest when we see it." Yet we do not love the highest either when we see it or when we hear it. In fact that is the real lesson Guinevere has learned when she speaks that thought. Truth just does not have its way willy-nilly with men. We have believed that we are charged to be truthful in what we say, and so we are—definitely and irrevocably charged to speak the truth as we know it. Nothing less than this will do; no equivocal, evasive, or subtly clever artistry will do!

Let that be understood, agreed upon, and held to be axiomatic!

Willie Willis stands before the mirror combing his hair and says, "I don't see why I have to go to Sunday school. I already know how to be better than I am." How long has Truth been in the World? Has she not been called "Time's Daughter"?[2] If we are not the first to proclaim it—if, indeed, one of our concerns is that we so lack originality—must we not look for another explanation of its delayed reign? Man's obtuseness cannot be the whole answer; his perverseness cannot bear more than its share of the blame. Truth in history is something like the words in a dictionary—in that form of mere existence they never make very thrilling reading.

Somewhere there is told the incident of the church dignitary meeting David Garrick and complaining that the theater reached the many, while the Church reached the few. Why was it, he asked, in view of their respective messages? Garrick is reported to have replied, "The reason, sir, is that we make Fiction appear to be true, while you speak Truth as though it were Fiction!"

Suppose we look briefly at some of the very obvious ways in which manner is more important than matter. First of all, there is the emphasis provided by punctuation. The classic example is the Prologue as spoken by the "rude mechanical" Quince, in Shakespeare's *Midsummer Night's Dream*.

> If we offend, it is with our good will.
>   That you should think, we come not to offend,
>   But with good will. To show our single skill,

[2] Samuel Butler, *Hudibras*.

> That is the true beginning of our end.
> Consider then, we come but in despite.
> We do not come, as minding to content you,
> Our true intent is. All for your delight,
> We are not here. That you should here repent you,
> The actors are at hand; and, by their show,
> You shall know all, that you are like to know.[8]

Dean Swift preached many sermons and wrote many political pamphlets, but which of them achieved the hearing of his *Gulliver's Travels?*

John Donne preached excellent sermons, but we remember better his "Holy Sonnets"—especially "Death Be Not Proud."

In the reporting of news, there are the newspaper, the radio, and the moving picture. In the newspaper there are the *Inquirer*, the *Christian Science Monitor*, the *Daily News* and the *Daily Worker*. In the recounting of history there are Toynbee, Latourette, the Bible, and the prevalent "comic-strip" method.

Suppose we wish to teach Christian truth—perhaps a lesson from the Bible. There has been a succession of methods even within our own spans of memory: Bible-centered, subject-centered, pupil-centered, and life-centered. There have been Bible lessons, Bible pictures, dramatizations, and now audio-visual-education. To discount any or to applaud any, may be really but a recognition of the superiority of manner to content.

Speaking of the Bible, why did the King James Version win and hold its position for so many centuries? Aside from all other more vital considerations, is there not one

[8] Act V, scene 1.

reason for its present lack of importance in its archaic language and its obsolete format?

One could go on and on to show how the form in which truth has appeared has conditioned its reception. To do so would be to court interruption by someone wishing to point out that lies, deception, and all manner of evil have achieved a hearing by the same means. The interruption and contention would be welcomed, agreed with, and added to the list of examples.

As soon as I had decided to write about the supremacy of style over truth in communication, I came across the same thing being said by so many others. Ivor Brown in *Shakespeare* writes:

> In our time we have had "the drama of ideas," and it was a welcome change from the fustian which it supplanted at a period when romanticism had run dry. But the conceptual and doctrinal drama will never have the general appeal possessed by the "ideas that are almost feelings." [4]

Lord David Cecil in the *Atlantic* for June, 1950, writes:

> There are authors who do not recognize the nature of their inspiration; and in consequence try to express it in a radically unsuitable form.
>
> [Some] fail to perceive the limitations of their medium. This is the chief cause of Wordsworth's notorious inequality. He did not realize that to put a statement into verse form gives it an emphasis, and that, therefore, it must be a statement that will bear emphasizing. As a result there is sometimes a comical incongruity between the prosaic flatness of what he says and the lilting song rhythm in which he says it:

[4] (London: Collins Press, 1949). pp. 284-85.

THE MAN WHO WOULD PREACH

For still the more he works, the more
Do his weak ankles swell.[5]

Form as a prerequisite of effective expression is observed in all the arts: poetry, fiction, drama, music, sculpture, and painting. Observe the necessary changes when one adapts a novel for the radio or movies; when an original violin solo is played on the saxophone; when the Lord's Prayer is interpreted by a rhythmic choir. All this is lands away from the conception of form that was evidenced by a student to whom I had just tried to explain the particular form of a particular poem. He replied, with a fine disregard for even the amenities, "I don't believe it. I think a poet just puts it in that form so that English teachers will have something to teach." Anyone who so summarily dismissed the sonnet, the triolet, the epic, and the ballad; anyone for whom there is no real difference between the rhymed couplet and blank verse; anyone who does not recognize that there is a difference between writing for the ear and writing for the eye, would probably see no difference between the Congressional Record and the *Iliad*.

Somerset Maugham writes in *The Summing Up* [6] of a Don's feeling:

Words should be used not only to balance a sentence, but to balance an idea. This is sound, for any idea may lose its effect if it is delivered abruptly. . . . An actor will sometimes say to an author: "Couldn't you give me a word or two more

[5] Vol. 185, No. 6, p. 76.

[6] Copyright 1938 by W. Somerset Maugham, reprinted by permission of Doubleday & Co., Inc , N. Y. and A. P. Watt & Son, London.

in this speech? It seems to take away all the point of my line if I have nothing else to say.

Later, speaking of the perfect prose of Dean Swift, he writes:

But perfection has one grave defect: It is apt to be dull. Swift's prose is like a French canal, bordered with poplars, that runs through a gracious and undulating country. Its tranquil charm fills you with satisfaction, but it neither excites the emotions nor stimulates the imagination. You go on and on and presently you are a trifle bored. So, much as you admire Swift's wonderful lucidity, his terseness, his naturalness, his lack of affectation, you find your attention wandering after a while unless his matter peculiarly interests you.

In the *Reader's Digest* for August, 1950, Rudolph Flesch writes an article he calls "Shirt-Sleeve English in One Easy Lesson." For this worthy enterprise he has devised four rules: 1. Go slow on rare and fancy words. 2. Don't worry too much about avoiding repetitions. 3. Don't worry too much about avoiding slang. 4. Don't worry too much about being grammatical. He adds, "It is now official that communication of thought is more important than correct grammar."

But suppose I do not want to speak "Shirt-Sleeve English"? And what if I am quite unimpressed by the pontifical statement that "It is now official"? And further suppose that I am slightly fanatical upon the fact that language is never just communication in the sense intended here? Where does all that leave Rudolph?

It left me scurrying to *Unpopular Opinions* by Dorothy

Sayers, and her particular essays "Plain English" and "The English Language." It was good to hear her demolish the contention that modern "telegraphese" is modern, clear and concise, vigorous, and economical of space. "Plain it is," she writes, "in the sense of ugly; but I think in no other." Considering the proper use of "shall" and "will,"

 . . . see how you can destroy the most beautiful parable in Scripture by using the one word for the other:

"I shall arise and go to my father and shall say unto him . . ."

How jaunty the words are now; how cocksure; how hypocritical; how they compel the sneering comment, "and the poor old blighter will fall for the sob-stuff again."

Then I turned to the letters of Lord Chesterfield and searched for the one "On Style." Here he writes:

Style is the dress of thoughts; and let them be ever so just, if your style is homely, coarse, and vulgar, they will appear to as much disadvantage, and be as ill received as your person, though ever so well proportioned, would, if dressed in rags, dirt and tatters.

Allow me here a brief interruption. At this point some will speak strongly against the Chesterfieldian implication, and will denounce the emptiness of the "elegances of style." They will quote Samuel Johnson's Prince Rasselas. The Prince found a philosopher who spoke great words of wisdom to him. Returning to him a few days later, he was told that the philosopher's daughter had died. The wise man was now a mourner, the victim of an utter despair that caused him to say,

EVEN MORE THAN TRUTH

What comfort can truth and reason afford me? Of what effect are they now, but to tell me that my daughter will not be restored?

The Prince, whose humanity would not suffer him to insult misery with reproof, went away, convinced of the emptiness of rhetorical sounds, and the inefficacy of polished periods and studied sentences.

My interpolation is to agree completely. Instead of disproving my thesis, it is grist for my mill.

This thought is more in the nature of a transition. It makes it easier for me to make my final proposal—namely, that we consider the perfect marriage of matter and manner. Gilbert and Sullivan will ever come to mind as the perfect marriage of words and music, which accounts for their survival beyond their contemporaneity.

On the other hand, the ineptitude of the following can hardly be overlooked—or, in my judgment, condoned. It is an attempt to dramatize Jesus for our present age. The first scene begins with the following conversation between Andrew and Philip:

Andrew: Hasn't this been a whale of a day!

Philip: Did you say holiday or helluva a day, Andy? If you said holiday you got me to lick!

Andrew: Phil, I couldn't lick a sick shrimp, much less a snappy shark like you. I'm all in. And you know I didn't say *holiday*. There ain't no such.

Perhaps that prepares you for the presentation of Jesus —and perhaps it doesn't. Herewith is a sampling of Jesus' language:

Congratulations, Jok! Glad to see you've junked those damned Roman adornments. Now you are really out of the chain-gang—for good and all I hope. (*Gives him the once-over.*) You are looking fine, old fellow! Feeling more like your old self, I reckon. . . . Perhaps that Hebrew beard of yours could stand a bit of trimming when you get home. John could fix you up in good Greek style if you were going to be around long enough. But at any rate he can tell you where you can get a razor. He uses one himself, you see. And he's converted half his comrades to the gospel of the clean face—and at least half converted me. (*To* John, *in answer to a suspicious look from him, followed by an appropriate gesture*) No, I didn't this morning or yesterday. Circumstances were against me. (*To* Peter, *who throughout this speech has been handling and is now feeling the edge of his sword*) Nice work, old swordfish! [7]

There is little left to be said. We have been given a message of magnificent stature and eternal significance. Our privilege of preaching it must be matched by our duty to preach it superbly—by our thought, word and gesture, and, most of all, by our spirit.

William Hamo Thornycroft, the English sculptor of the nineteenth century, was a friend of Edmund Gosse. He entered the competition for a statue of William Harvey, sponsored by the Royal College of Physicians. His entry was rejected; entry "B" won the award. In a letter to Thornycroft, Gosse wrote, "It would be a thousand times worse to have made B than to lose the award."

Five months later, in another letter to the sculptor, Gosse has this to say:

[7] Mercer Green Johnston, *The First Among the Unafraid* (Washington, D.C.: The Longwood Co., 1947) , pp. 2, 43.

It seems to me that in Sculpture more depends on the subject than in painting: since in painting, you may give real artistic pleasure by rendering the bloom on a cabbage-garden or the light on a bundle of chimney-stacks, but somehow if you employ so splendid and eternal a medium as marble it seems as though you need more than mere admirable workmanship, you want the elevation of some really (and not merely relatively) beautiful idea.[8]

At the risk of seeming to be only multiplying quotations I should like to introduce the evidence of two more writers. Harold Holson, the London dramatic critic of *The Christian Science Monitor,* reviewed a performance given in England of the cycle of Shakespearean Kings, during the course of which he made a most pertinent observation.

Important as the technical reasources of a playhouse are, the company matters even more. Sir Cedric Hardwicke says he would rather hear a first-rate actor recite the railway time-table than listen to amateurs in the best play in the world; and I would prefer seeing Kean in a barn to watching even a moderately good company on the stage of the Metropolitan Opera or Drury Lane, or whatever is the last word in wealth and sumptuosity.[9]

This is a truth particularly pertinent to preaching and the church because it clearly reveals the fact that communication is also personal, and the sermon is also the man preaching it. He must be "a vessel for noble use, consecrated and useful to the master of the house, ready for any good work." He must also have a competence in the han-

[8] Evan Charteris, *The Life and Letters of Sir Edmund Gosse* (New York: Harper & Bros., 1931), pp. 110-111.
[9] August 10, 1951, sec. 2, p. 9.

dling of his tools, for preaching requires the preacher to be both artist and artisan.

The second writer is Margery Allingham, the novelist. We all know that the greatest art is the concealment of art. Let her be plain spoken and brilliant. "I write every paragraph four times," she says, "once to get my meaning down, once to put in anything I left out, once to take out anything that seems unnecessary, and once to make the whole thing sound as if I had only just thought of it."

As we have said, all this may seem to have been but the offering of the words of others to say what is desired to be said. It has been intentionally more. It has been an extended illustration of the basic contention that the way in which a truth is spoken may be at least as important as the truth itself—both in the matter of communication and for the effective reception by a hearer. Style and manner are the indisputable media for the adequate transference of matter. What we have been doing is to allow others to say what we wanted said, because they did it so superlatively, and their manner of stating the truth made the choice of their statements easy and promising. We are in no sense thinking of style merely in terms of the fanciful ornateness of obscurantism. One does not use the same words, the same grammar, the same style in urging his home team on to victory that one uses in prayer to God—at least he should not. Nor should one reverse the process. In each case there is a compatible style of speech; and only ignorance or pretense will prefer the one when the other is normal procedure—normal and therefore effective.

Therefore, the first thing to be said about the manner of our preaching is that it must be the manner best suited to the occasion. This takes study, and supersedes any reliance upon that much-overvalued gift of native ability or its weaker counterpart the "gift of gab." Whenever I have a student who does excellent work by relying solely upon what he brought to the Seminary and happily accepts the undiscerning approval of his audience, I am always hurt, and long to urge him to consider what he could do if he were to add to whatever he felt he had been blest with, that worthy increment of discipline and knowledge. Heaven help the preacher who thinks that only heaven can help him!

The second thing that may be said as a result of our quotations is that they never would have been selected in the first place, or remembered by anyone who read them, unless they won that attention by the very fact we have been trying to establish—their style of presenting the truth.

Finally, those who preach must again note the proverb referred to earlier, "A word fitly spoken is like apples of gold in a setting of silver" (Prov. 25:11). The apples are gold and the setting is silver—and perhaps for the moment that is a proper statement of their respective values—but both are precious metals according to the judgment of the maxim's author. One's imagination may easily provide a corollary in which the word unfitly spoken may still be apples of gold, but in a setting that dulls and cheapens both itself and the word. Even Jesus was characterized on one occasion as being noted for the way he spoke: "he taught them as one who had authority, and not as their scribes." (Matt. 7:29). And this, you will remember, was the climactic word for the Sermon on the Mount.

Yes, the way in which we speak the truth is important.

71

THE MAN WHO WOULD PREACH

If the Word of Life is man's most important and greatest possession, and the preaching of it his highest privilege, then, indeed, he cannot keep faith even with himself if he handle it carelessly and preach it in a shabby manner. Apples of gold demand a silver setting.

Even when we have come to some approximation of a satisfying combination of matter and manner, we shall find ourselves once again the victims of an ever-recurring sense of futility. How can we possibly do justice to the theme of our preaching? Will it not always be "The Galilean Too Great"? There is a word of promise in a conversation between two characters of Hawthorne's *The Marble Faun*. Kenyon, the sculptor, has just completed his statue of Cleopatra, and an inevitable reaction has set in. He has come to the time when, he says:

I look at what I fancied to be a statue, lacking only breath to make it live, and find it a mere heap of senseless stone, into which I have not really succeeded in moulding the spiritual part of my idea. . . . I should like to hit poor Cleopatra a bitter blow on her Egyptian nose with this mallet.

His friend Hilda reminds him that he must not be too much disheartened by the decay of his faith in what he has produced.

I have heard a poet express similar distaste for his own most exquisite poems, and I am afraid that this final despair, and sense of short-coming, must always be the reward and punishment of those who try to grapple with a great or beautiful idea. It only proves that you have been able to imagine things too high for mortal faculties to execute.

Chapter V

The Liberality of Adventure

The proper person to discuss preaching and the sermon would seem to be the preacher. That is why the *Encyclopedia Britannica* holds 'a surprise for us. The article on preaching *is* by a preacher, Alexander James Grieve. The surprise comes in the article on the sermon. The author is a distinguished man of letters and literary critic, a contributor of many articles to the ninth edition and the chief literary advisor of the tenth and eleventh editions of the *Britannica*, Edmund Gosse. The implication—and I believe it is a valid one—is that the sermon is a distinct literary form. This position is verified in the article when Gosse writes, "Since the end of the eighteenth century . . . although the pulpit holds its own in Protestant and Catholic countries alike, for purposes of exhortation and encouragement, it cannot be said that the sermon has in any way extended its influence as a form of pure literature." Although Gosse is pre-eminently a man of letters, he is by no means a poor choice to write about the sermon, as readers of his *Father and Son* and those who have studied his life well know.

After highly commending the sermons of Augustine he writes, "His object was not to dazzle by a conformity with the artificial rules of oratory, but to move the soul of the listener by a direct appeal to his conscience." From this it would appear that the preaching of a sermon is the artistic presentation of a religious theme for the express purpose of effecting a closer relationship between God and the hearers. Indeed, I wish to offer this as a working definition.

Like all definitions it has terms that need themselves to be defined. It allows anyone to choose one or more of the words, like artistic, religious, relationship and God, and to dispute their relevance or their meaning. Such a dispute or questioning may be genuine and important, but it may just as easily be merely a debating trick or a somewhat willful evasion. It is easier to challenge the meaning of another man than to work through to a meaning of our own.

The most important fact about this definition, however, is that it has remained the basic contention upon which all preaching has been done. Throughout the history of the Christian Church those who preached sermons were doing so because they believed in its statements. True, they had their varying ideas of the meanings of the very words we have chosen as possible points of challenge. The idea of God held by one age was certainly not the idea held by an earlier age; the experience and the fact of the relationship between God and man, with the inevitable introduction of a concept of salvation, have not remained static. Moreover, the definition leaves unmentioned the results of an achieved relationship with God—results that are essential to any modern conception of the Christian life. We cannot today even consider a religious life that suggests merely the ascetic; and the practical world of the twentieth century makes inevitable our demand that religion be expressed in the social order. Yet the main stream of Christian preaching has always flowed from God to the people for the purposes of enlightening, encouraging, and empowering them to fuller living.

One factor of all Christian preaching is to be noticed: it proclaims a message with authority. The authority has varied with the ages. It began as the life and teachings of Jesus—substantiated by and from the Old Testament—moved through the Scriptures, the Church, back to the Scriptures, to a form of personal experience. One of the frequent weaknesses of Christian preaching is the absence of an authority anything like one of these. We grope for a message that will be all things to all men, careful not to antagonize the cultured, nor to estrange the educated. We lay out the way of life, but conscious that it may cross other people's property and fearful of the resultant condemnation, we are most likely to end with a tortuous, narrow lane that submissively follows the contour of the land over which it goes. Thus we are liberal in our considerations or considerateness, but lack the liberality of adventure.

This loss of authority and general mildness in conviction are joined by a dilemma in the matter of the province of the Church. On the one hand, if we concentrate upon a peculiar character of the Church; as for example, worship, and preach a distinctly God-centered sermon, we are aware of the justice of the accusation that we leave so much untouched. We are reminded that all the modern cults have arisen to meet the genuine needs of those people who were denied satisfaction within the restricted ministry of the Church.

On the other hand, if we set out to fight along the whole

battle line of human warfare, we are again reminded that we spread our forces too thinly, and will do far better to concentrate them at the one sector that is peculiarly ours. Indeed, the modern revival of worship is a comment upon and a reaction to our previous misdirection, just as our more modern revival of biblical theology is another rebuke. The dilemma is not easily resolved. It is very pointed in the comparison of English with American preaching. Joseph Fort Newton writes in his *River of Years:*

> In intellectual average and moral passion there is little difference between English and American preaching, but the emphasis is dissimilar.
> The English preacher seeks to educate and edify his people in the fundamentals of faith and duty; the American preacher is more intent upon the application of religion to the affairs of the moment. The Englishman goes to church, as to a house of ancient mystery, to forget the turmoil of the world, to refresh his spirit, to regain the great backgrounds of life, against which he may see the problems of the morrow. It is said that the distinctive note of the American pulpit is vitality; of the English pulpit, serenity. In the one more activism, in the other more otherworldliness. Perhaps each has something to learn from the other.[1]

Although this was written some ten years ago, it is just as true today.

My own conviction is that the answer lies in the direction of a concentration of the message and the distribution of its application. That is, the sermon is a God-centered message that moves the hearers to a world-consciousness and a

[1] (Philadelphia: J. B. Lippincott Co., 1946), p. 151. Used by permission of the publisher.

world-effective life. The two laws that are one still remain the same—and in the same order: "Love the Lord thy God . . . and thy neighbor . . . ."

The age in which we live has characteristics that present peculiar problems to religion. No age has allowed religion to go unchallenged, and the attacks in our day are vigorous and definitely prescribed—the most devastating being that of science. It seems trite and old-fashioned to drag out this old bugaboo; one faces the likelihood of being character- ized as out-of-date, unaware that the world has moved be- yond such puerile antagonism. That the conflict generally has been recognized and resolved is largely true in specific instances, but absolutely false in its general aspects. Actual- ly there is and always will be—because there must be—at least a division of labor between science and religion, just as there is between science and art, and science and litera- ture. The fields of operation are different; the procedures vary, and the principles and purposes are distinct. Any synthesis lies in the individual to which each makes its contribution; together they move toward a whole man.

In our day the advances of science have been tremendous and overpowering in their influences upon life. Our un- derstanding of the natural world has increased beyond our comprehension, beyond our ability to assimilate into everyday knowledge and use. One man comments, "We have become educated beyond our intelligence"; another quotes Thoreau: "Our inventions are wont to be pretty toys, which distract our attention from serious things. They are but improved means to an unimproved end, an end which it was already but too easy to arrive at; as rail- roads lead to Boston or New York." While this has its profound effect upon what we believe, it goes beyond the facts to what essentially is a discrediting of the sources of our previous knowledge. That is, our conception of God has been forced into narrower limits; his domain becomes smaller and smaller, his power less and less, and, consequently, his authority approaches the vanishing point altogether. Modern religious man has become a perfect parallel of that ancient carpenter who

heweth him down cedars, and taketh the cypress and the oak, . . . He burneth part thereof in the fire; with part thereof he eateth flesh; he roasteth roast, and is satisfied; yea, he warmeth himself, and saith, Aha, I am warm, I have seen the fire: and the residue thereof he maketh a god. (Isa. 44:14, 16-17.)

This would be important in itself, but more follows. Science has properly gone beyond the natural world to that of the personal and social. Not merely the stars, the rocks, and the elements come under its scrutiny, but man himself is an object of its investigations. Thus, the newest and most fascinatingly persuasive of the sciences is our immediate inheritance—psychiatry. The last stronghold of religion has been invaded and every minister is girding up his loins, or at least he was until Freud was modified. The present-day function of the minister as a pastor is as old as religion itself, but today it savors somewhat of an attempt to retain a prerogative. When the minister is not being warned of just how far he can legitimately go as a psychiatrist, he is being comforted by the assurance that religion still plays an important part in the rehabilitation of the person. In any event, he is on the defensive again;

the words "He restoreth my soul" are in the Bible, aren't they?

Yet even as one says "in the Bible," another problem presents itself. In religion we, too, have made scientific advances. Our most recent sciences have concerned themselves with critical investigations of sources and ascriptions. Comparative religion joins hands with historical criticism to assure us that we also have the scientific spirit and courage, and that truth is our main objective. The uniqueness of Christianity has disappeared; the foundations of our authoritative pronouncements have been excavated and instead of a solid rock, we have discovered that our particular island of interest is built upon what resembles a coral reef, the porous conglomeration of the skeletons of earlier life.

The whole picture is that of the faltering, unsure gropings of those who came from a line of priests, but hesitatingly admit that they may now be but little more than acolytes at the altars of an ancient fire. The situation is not so much a confusion in details, as a wavering in spirit. For too many preachers it is not a matter of being a member of the shock troops, but of being merely replacements.

If this were the problem of the clergy alone, it would be enough, but it is also the problem of the laity. The preacher does not speak into the echo chamber of his own thoughts, but in the church, and to a congregation, however small that congregation may be. Preaching is not merely speaking—it is speaking to people, and the condition and attitude of the people are definitely a part of the whole problem, as well as of its solution. Our people have been a part of our world of science, knowledge, and progress; they have been conditioned by the same advances we have known. What is more, they have listened to us, and have detected the note of doubtful or even complaining assent that we have given to the new world, the foreign accent of one not quite familiar with the tongue he speaks, the grudging admission of confusion, the belligerent controversy about minutiae, the skittish evasion of the essentials. Coming from the difficulties of their own world, the congregation finds that they have but entered into another world of doubt. Beset by a needful search for realities and power, they discover the keen disappointment of loss at the very place where they had rightfully expected to find authority and assurance. If that trumpet speaks with an uncertain voice, who shall prepare himself for battle?

The delivery of a sermon then is more—far more—than merely speaking to a group of people. Preaching involves the consideration of five elements. In the first place, there is the occasion—a church-worship service. Lest this be thought too obvious to need note, observe how a natural distinction is made by many between a morning and an evening service and between a Sunday and a midweek service. The character of the address varies with each occasion, because both the speaker and the hearers recognize a difference in the mood and expectation. The service of worship demands an address that is more carefully prepared to be consistent with the experience of worship; the expectancy is that of establishing a closer relationship to God; the objective is the development of the religious nature of the hearers, which will eventuate in an outward expression of the new conviction and feelings. Belief and emotion bring about resolution.

Second, the hearers are not an audience, but a congregation. The theater plays to an audience; those who attend have little that brought them together beyond the immediate experience they anticipate; there is no distinctive community experience. After the play the audience disperses to their several situations with no interdependent relationship of purpose involved in the time they spent together. A play that is propaganda or has a "purpose" is not good drama. A church service gathers a congregation—people brought together by a common assent to the suppositions of the church, by precedent conditions of relationship—and they are dismissed with the implications and the obligations of the hour spent together still upon them. Generally they do not lose their social identification with the pronouncement of the benediction.

Third, the speaker is not a visitor but a fellow. He lives with the people, ministers beyond the limits of the hour, serves in various capacities, and is one among them. His obligations are for the whole of their lives, not for the promptings of the moment. What he says in the pulpit is heeded, not for intrinsic truth or applicability alone, but only as a part of his larger ministry. The Obadiah Slopes will always be told by the Madeline Nerones: "As for me, I will believe in no belief that does not make itself manifest by outward signs. I will think no preaching sincere that is not recommended by the practice of the preacher." [2] It is true that the sermon is not an entity in itself, but only a part of the preaching of the preacher. Thus, the whole character of the preacher speaks in any one sermon. His attitude toward people, his conception of his task, his

[2] Anthony Trollope, *Barchester Towers*, ch. xxvii.

81

manner and his very soul enter into a sermon and often the people believe they are condemning his theology when they are really resenting his character; they may agree with what he says, but heartily object to the way he says it. They will often accept ignorance spoken kindly, and reject the truth uttered belligerently and sarcastically. It is unfortunate, but the result is often the further propagation of the false and the inadequate; while truth gets no hearing and is even discredited because of the distastefulness of its bearer. It is not enough to speak the truth; it must be spoken in kindness.

Fourth, the sermon—to repeat—is not a neatly parceled segment of truth delivered by a messenger who gets a receipt for its delivery, and goes away unconcerned for anything beyond the satisfaction occasioned by the completion of his own personal obligation. He has delivered the goods; the further disposition of the matter is in the hands of the receiver. Too often the truth is exactly that— in the hands of the receiver. "Truth crushed to earth will rise again," but a package of truth crushed by the careless handling of the messenger is often thrown into the wastebin. Perhaps there is no inexorable demand that the sermon be accepted, but necessity is laid upon the preacher to deliver it acceptably. His is not an ecclesiastical program of "Take It or Leave It," but probably comes nearer to being "One Man's Family."

He is not the preacher of a sermon, but the pastor of the people, and the sermon is a means, not an end. Let him never forget that! His work is not finished when the sermon is concluded; it only begins. In fact, the true ministry may begin only when the sermon is finished. The preacher may well test his efficiency by frank answers to such questions as: Did that sermon make the elements of religion—God, prayer, the church—more real to the hearer? Did it create in the hearers a desire to conform to its truth? Did it make it easier for them to talk with me about their religious living? Did it make religion available? In brief, the criterion is not "Was it a good sermon?" but did it do good?; not "Did I preach well?" but will the people be better for having heard it?

Finally, the nature and content of the sermon itself are of paramount importance. If it is to meet the demands previously stated for consideration, it must have a character consistent with these requirements and it must apply itself to them. Therefore, it is not an essay, a lecture, a paper, or a thesis. Neither is it a pep talk, a sales talk, or a jolly discussion of life. The sermon is still the word of God, spoken to the people of God by the servant of God. It uses knowledge and intelligence, emotion and feeling, and experience, but does not make them the criteria of preaching. These, again, are means, not ends. Because it is a thing of beauty, like all art, it is a joy forever. Like poetry it finds the general in the specific and shows the great sweeping tides of the universal in the particular. It is, to speak religiously, God among us. The sermon is not the preacher's solutions to life's problems, but his humble sharing with fellow travelers of the signs he has read, the experiences he has found so useful, the revelation—and the word is not peculiarly religious or sacrosanct—the revelation of God.

The word "emotion" has been used earlier. At this point it may be well to say something in defense of this abused

and maligned quality of a good sermon. It has been done
well by C. S. Lewis in a series of lectures on *The Abolition
of Man, or Reflections on Education with Special Reference to the Teaching of English in the Upper Forms of
Schools.* He is speaking about an author who debunks a
silly bit of writing on horses without adding anything of
the genuine love of horses as a substitute. He is distressed
at such people.

They see the world around them swayed by emotional propaganda—they have learned from tradition that youth is sen-
timental—and they conclude that the best thing they can do
is to fortify the minds of young people against emotion. My
own experience as a teacher tells me an opposite tale. For
every pupil who needs to be guarded from a weak excess of
sensibility there are three who need to be awakened from the
slumber of cold vulgarity. The task of the modern educator
is not to cut down jungles but to irrigate deserts. The right
defence against false sentiments is to inculcate just sentiments.
By starving the sensibility of our pupils we only make them
easier prey to the propagandist when he comes. For famished
nature will be avenged and a hard heart is no infallible pro-
tection against a soft head.[3]

If one wishes a shorter comment, it is provided by Uncle
Toby in Laurence Sterne's *Tristram Shandy.* Corporal
Trim has just finished reading the famous Sermon on
Conscience and has remarked, "I should have read it ten
times better, . . . but that my heart was so full." Uncle
Toby replies:

That was the very reason, Trim, . . . which has made thee

[3] (New York: the Macmillan Co., 1947), pp. 8-9. Used by permission of
the publisher, the Macmillan Co., and Geoffrey Bles, Ltd., London.

read the sermon as well as thou hast done; and if the clergy of our Church, . . . would take part in what they deliver, as deeply as this poor fellow has done—as their compositions are fine; . . . the eloquence of our pulpits, with such subjects to inflame it—would be a model for the whole world—But, alas; . . . like *French* politicians in this respect, what they gain in the cabinet they lose in the field.

Preaching is a form of communication and, therefore, one of the arts. Lest that word "art" conjure up fantastic pictures of a pulpit Bunthorne, let it be remembered that an art is merely "the skillful and systematic arrangement or adaptation of means for the attainment of some end." Our problem, then, is merely the age-old one of all arts. A picture, a poem, or a musical composition is an idea or an experience plus a means of communication. The medium of communication is at least as important as the idea—sometimes more important. Take so simple a situation as our desire to express our sympathy to one who has lost a child. Who has not written, "I wish I had words to express my sympathy"? While sympathy can never be put completely and adequately into any words, our statement of the difficulty is in part a matter of our own inability to command the medium properly. Have we not also wished ` we could paint a picture of some impressive scene of beauty? Who has not marveled at the facility of expression of those who have mastered the media of gold and silver, of copper and bronze?

So with religion that is to be conveyed to others by words. Again a simple example will illustrate. To anyone familiar with the first two verses of Genesis in the King James Version, the following translation made by Ferrer

Fenton, will indicate at least the source of the material translated: "By periods God created that which produced the Suns; then that which produced the Earth. But the Earth was unorganised and empty; and darkness covered its convulsed surface; but the breath of God vibrated over its fluid face." Nor am I impressed by the translator's introductory note, at the end of which he states: "My work is the most accurate rendering into any European language, ancient or modern, ever made, not only in words, but in editing, spirit and sense. I contend that I am the only man who has ever applied real mental literary criticism to the Sacred Scriptures."

The cold facts of a scientific and rationalized conclusion are usually quite devoid of any beauty; that quality comes only after the mind and the heart have had an opportunity to turn them over in experience, allow the light of significant form to play upon them and, by the thus acquired better acquaintance with them, feel friendly and warm toward their overtones. This cannot be done with something absolutely new. Eugene O'Neil could not do it with *Dynamo;* the cubists could not do it with art; the intellectual school of poets could not do it with visual poems. Neither can the minister do it. He must wait until the power *behind* the facts, joins with the power *of* the facts to give a real and lasting impetus *to* the facts. That is, he must learn to distinguish between that which he lays hold on and that which lays hold upon him. It is not a new vocabulary we need, but a new rhetoric and a new poetry.

Mary Webb in *The Spring of Joy* has a word to say that subtly characterizes our problem, as well as deftly suggests the solution:

Nature sets her dances to every rhythm, from slow undulations to the swift, dangerous rushes that bring wild exhilaration. The long pendulum-swing of trees is restful, not in the ambitious manner of quiescence—that might mean death; nor with the sudden cessation of movement—that might mean injury; but with the content of a return after swaying out to a fixed place, which implies balance and vitality. In the same way a poised mind sweeps out to all new ideas, but is not torn from its place because of its roots.

What, then, is the conclusion of the matter? What is our thesis for the present-day preacher? First, our concern is for the preacher rather than for preaching, which is always secondary. The man comes first; what he does is a natural sequence. Therefore the desired end is not to produce an education but an educated person. We must take our cue from the state examination for an automobile driver's license. It includes questions about the mechanism and operation of the automobile, the meaning of the signs along the road, and the laws of the state, but it does not stop there. There are also questions about the moral character and social responsibility of the driver. The applicant is examined as a man! Only to one who can satisfactorily answer this last demand is there given a license to drive— and only one who continues to answer satisfactorily can keep it.

Second, critical study may lead to critical philosophy, even to cynicism. The fault is not with the material. The initial thrill of even genuine discovery is not a sufficient warrant for an immediate official pronouncement. One needs to remember the preacher in the chapel of whom Browning speaks:

THE MAN WHO WOULD PREACH

No sooner our friend had got an inkling
Of treasure hid in the Holy Bible,

.   .   .   .

Than he handled it so, in fine irreverence,
As to hug the book of books to pieces.[4]

Such a one might well have considered the admonition of
Holmes: "Talk about those subjects you have had long in
your mind, and listen to what others say about subjects
you have studied but recently. Knowledge and timber
shouldn't be used till they are seasoned." The neophyte is
often as ridiculous a figure as Archimedes is reputed to
have been when he, too, shouted "Eureka!" too soon after
his discovery.

Finally, the preacher is a man of religion, always remembering that he is to speak within the life area of religion. That is, he uses facts for a purpose; he emphasizes
techniques for an impression. He must give to his hearers
not merely a sense of intellectual achievement, but also an
experience of the mystery of God. Religion, like the arts,
concerns itself with the imponderables, by which one lives
as surely as he does by the things he encompasses. A sermon
should leave the hearer with another portion of life over
which he has become the master, but also with a vision of
life to which he becomes the servant. He must see Life beyond his comprehension, toward which he purposes to
journey under the compulsions of faith and with the reas-
onable expectancy of hope.

When we preach that kind of sermon, some new Chaucer
will write of some new Good Parson!

[4] "Christmas Eve," sec. 3.

Chapter VI

The Riddle of the Sermon

Almost everything that needs to be said about preaching, was said in the first lectures by Henry Ward Beecher that opened that remarkable series bearing his distinguished family name. Reading them again almost discourages one who would speak or write about the task of preaching. Beecher's lectures and his answers to questions asked him at the conclusion of each lecture give us again and again an insight into the truths that the subsequent years seem only to have confirmed. In the third lecture of the first series called "The Personal Element in Oratory," he says there are different classes of hearers.

No man ever preaches, . . . without very soon being made conscious that men are so different from each other that no preaching will be continuously effective which is not endlessly various; and that not for the sake of arresting attention, but because all men do not take in moral teaching by the same sides of their minds.

Some men will never be led except through the reason. He continues,

Yet, if you shape your preaching, as often literary men in the pulpit are accustomed to do, to the distinctively intellectual men in the community, you will very soon fill them full and starve the rest of your congregation; because, right alongside of them, there are natures just as noble as theirs, but not accustomed to receive their food through the mouth of reason, except in an incidental and indirect way. . . .

The man who means to catch men, and to catch all of them, must prepare bait for those that bite purely by the understanding, and just as much bait for those that bite largely by their emotions.

The whole lecture should be read, even at the risk of your temptation to quote sentence after sentence to the next preacher you meet. There are sentences like, "If a man can be saved by pure intellectual preaching, let him have it," and

take men as it has pleased God to make them; and let your preaching, so far as concerns the selection of material, and the mode and method by which you are presenting the truth, follow the wants of the persons themselves, and not simply the measure of your own minds.

How true this is—that we have a wide variety of people before us whenever and wherever we preach, and to complicate matters the more, each individual is a small crowd of persons within himself. How shall we preach to this potential multitude? Indeed, how can we? Among the many possible variations that present themselves to us, let us concentrate our attention on the variations in age —and we mean chronological age with all its accompanying characteristics.

It requires no memory at all to recall the relatively recent interest in the child, as it requires no observation to see the present interest in old age. Pediatrics and geriatrics —the very words are the prized possessions of pastor and seminary student. We have our educational buildings as the joint project of the architect and the director of religious education. Our old folks are now firmly established in the bibliography of counseling. What then of our preaching? Shall we not be equally alert to the necessity for at least as varied a homiletical meal as we have learned to serve on the dining-room table? Is it any longer wise for us to preach the word with a fierce disregard for its acceptability on the part of the hearers? Can we justify our contention that it is our task to present the truth and our congregation's part to receive what we preach—a privilege they neglect or disregard at their own risk, both temporal and eternal? Hardly! It is not enough to preach the word, nor even to preach the word in love; it must also be preached in kind.

The very statement about "speaking the truth in love" is part of an injunction to grow up, be mature, recognize that we must no longer be children, but adults with an adult's advantages. This, we need hardly say, is the same man who wrote an even better known distinction between the child and the man, with a very clear statement of the very sure differences. The child is not merely a small adult, any more than the mature man is merely a grown child. Wordsworth's "the child is father of the man" asserts this truth, and our accusations of "adult infantilism" prove it. We know there is a difference—and an important one—even when we do not act upon our knowledge. Act upon it we should, especially in our preaching.

Of course, the admission that we ought to do so if we are to preach effectively is much easier admitted than accomplished. It probably is not the fashion nowadays to read so outmoded a book as *Dream-Life* by Ik. Marvel (Donald G. Mitchell), but it might well serve a purpose for the preacher who needs to be reminded that there are seasons of life as well as of the year. If we must read only a single chapter from the book, for this present occasion let it be "Boy Religion" with its beginning: "Is my weak soul frightened that I should write of the religion of the boy?"

It acknowledges an awareness of the feeling on the part of some

that the subject may not be approached except through the dicta of certain ecclesiastic bodies, and that the language which touches it must not be that every-day language which mirrors the vitality of our thought, but should have some twist of that theologic mannerism, which is as cold to the boy as to the busy man of the world.

Quietly the essay continues mincing no words but speaking the truth in love, asking us to see the boy as a boy, willing to listen, even to believe, what his elders say and preach, but terribly baffled by their seeming aloofness from his world of work and play. And then the concluding paragraph:

Is it absurd to suppose that some adaptation is desirable? And might not the teachings of that Religion, which is the aegis of our moral being, be inwrought with some of those finer harmonies of speech and form which were given to wise ends —and lure the boyish soul by something akin to that gentleness which belonged to the Nazarene Teacher, and which provided not only meat for men, but "milk for babes"? [1]

Again it was Paul who has given us precedent in his "Declaration of Dependence":

For though I am free from all men, I have made myself a slave to all, that I might win the more. To the Jews I became as a Jew, in order to win Jews; to those under the law I became as one under the law—though not being myself under the law—that I might win those under the law. To those outside the law I became as one outside the law—not being without law toward God but under the law of Christ—that I might win those outside the law. To the weak I became weak, that I might win the weak. I have become all things to all men, that I might by all means save some. I do it all for the sake of the gospel, that I may share in its blessings. (I Cor. 9:19-23.)

And let no one omit the first or the last sentence in that statement!

Paul is saying that he has put himself in the place of every man he would help, understanding him before he would direct him. (Isn't our modern word for it "empathy"?) Dare we do otherwise?

One of the surest and clearest revelations of the differences existing among us in matters of religious sensitiveness is in an experience that probably every one of us has had at least once—and no doubt many times. We read a very familiar part of the Bible and suddenly, like a revelation, comes an idea, a feeling or an understanding we have never before seen in what we have just read. It is like

---

[1] Used by permission of the Publisher, The Bobbs-Merrill Co., Inc.

Keats' "On First Looking into Chapman's Homer"—a whole new world flashes into our view and we stand "silent, upon a peak in Darien."

Perhaps this is one of the best recommendations for reading the Bible in one of the modern translations; surely it is one of the best results. The King James Version reads: "Charity suffereth long, and is kind; charity envieth not; charity vaunteth not itself, is not puffed up. Doth not behave itself unseemly, seeketh not her own, is not easily provoked, thinketh no evil." (1 Cor. 13:4-5.) Noble thoughts nobly expressed, and too often only nobly believed. Then one day we read the same verses in the Revised Standard Version. "Love is patient and kind; love is not jealous or boastful; it is not arrogant or rude. Love does not insist on its own way; it is not irritable or resentful." What a difference that makes!

We are more familiar with patience than with long-suffering; with boastfulness than with vaunting oneself; and certainly the single words "arrogant" and "rude" carry a picture and a consequent conviction not communicated by the phrases "puffed up" and "behave itself unseemly." We may have some trouble identifying the person who seeketh his own, but we know immediately the one who insists upon having his own way.

For an even greater difference and consequently greater impressiveness, read this same portion in *Letters to Young Churches* by J. B. Phillips. His is an English translation about which I, as Alexander Woollcott said he frequently did, have "gone quietly mad." This version has it as:

This love of which I speak is slow to lose patience—it looks for a way of being constructive. It is not possessive; it is neither anxious to impress nor does it cherish inflated ideas of its own importance.

Love has good manners and does not pursue selfish advantage. It is not touchy.[2]
The difference now is not merely one of language; it has become one of experience.

In the same way, as we grow older, we can call upon more and different experiences to interpret the mere words of the Bible. As we mentioned earlier, we now have silver frames for our golden apples. The preacher must remember that it is in this sense too that he preaches to the varied ages.

Let us take it from another angle. For the different ages of man—are there seven—there are different meanings for what is apparently the same word. Thus, though all seek goals, the goals themselves differ. Ask a boy what he is going to be when he grows up, and to his adult questioner the answer is far from conclusive or even accurate. We are more inclined to treat it good humoredly, with the sure knowledge that, fortunately for us, not all the boys who say so really do grow up to be policemen, detectives, spacemen, and comedians. Did your high-school class publish a book in which appeared your picture and a sketch of your life to that point, with a statement either of your choice of a future or the prediction of your class prophet? Have you looked at it recently?

One's capacities also vary. Physically, mentally, and socially what we can endure, assimilate, or appropriate varies from age to age. Some of us are thankful that we no longer

[a] (New York: The Macmillan Co., 1947), p. 60.

have to chin ourselves even once to prove our right to respect. There comes a time, too, when we can be heard for
the quality rather than the quantity of our reading. The
way we prove that we are "able" changes with the chronological age. Fortunately our satisfactions alter, and what
pleases at twenty is not likely to please at forty. (If it does,
a psychiatrist may be indicated.) The deeper satisfactions
come with the passing of time, and we are made richer
by the wealth of experience. A woman of fifty does not
find the satisfactions she once found in the compliments of
an earlier day; she thinks them slightly ridiculous. The
adult man truly puts away childish things—things of the
heart and mind as well as of the playroom.

Elizabeth Gray Vining chose the title of her book from
the instructions given by those who asked her to under-
take the education of the Crown Prince of Japan. "We
want you," they said, "to open for him windows on a
wider world." And it became so, *Windows for the Crown
Prince*. The same instructions are for every child who
would inherit the Kingdom of Heaven. Windows—one of
which should be a "Daniel's Window."

As if to complicate matters still further, even when
we evidence the same attitude toward life, we show it
toward different objects. All ages are skeptical, but not
about the same things. Our doubts change from age to
age, and we wonder why we even doubted as youth, what
age has proved to be so certain. We fear, but how different
are our fears! From the darkness of the room we go to the
darkness of the world; from fears of the unknown, to fears
of the known. Man has been curious, and that has often
taught him safety, and brought him health. The questions

of "what" and "where" give way to "how," which finally surrenders to the greatest question of all, "why?" It has been said that the shortest poem in the English language is:

I!

Why?

What of our needs? "Man wants but little here below, Nor wants that little long," is poetry—not fact. Indeed, a President of the United States took issue with it and wrote,

> "Man wants but little here below,
>   Nor wants that little long,"
> 'Tis not with me exactly so;
>   But 'tis so in the song.
> My wants are many and, if told,
>   Would muster quite a score;
> And were each wish a mint of gold,
>   I still should long for more.[3]

The writers of advertising seem to agree to a man with the President. They are sure that we have a multitude of wants and needs, and they have taught us to disregard any alleged difference between the two. If we want it, we need it. If it is true that the wants of a man about a hundred years ago totaled seventy-two, of which sixteen were necessities, would anyone dare to estimate what a century has done to those figures? Well, did Emerson say, "Want is a growing giant whom the coat of Have was never large enough to cover."

[3] John Quincy Adams, "The Wants of Man."

THE MAN WHO WOULD PREACH

Again we ask: What then of preaching? How do we
speak to this hydra-headed, insatiable subject called the
congregation? Is the task not simply Herculean, but impossible? Yes, in a sense it is impossible. We ought to
admit that freely, and so rid ourselves of the embarrass-
ment of trying and the humility of failing. But it is necessary that we preach; and we ought equally to admit that,
and so save ourselves the greater humility of not trying at
all. The paradox of preaching is that it is impossible to
do, even while it is also impossible for the preacher not
to try to do!

The fact that there are so many moods and tempers reveals a commanding truth: that one kind of preaching—
whatever that kind is—is ultimately inadequate to meet
all needs. We are often told, "Don't talk wisdom, talk
comfort! Remember there are hurt souls in your congregation. If you have a 'good' sermon, you will do no good."
This is the half-truth that points toward the whole truth.
If we continually preach only to those who need comfort,
we fail to reach those who need to be challenged, warned,
or taught. It is just as bad to have a false sense of comfort as to have a sense of false comfort. A concert soloist or
a symphony conductor makes up a program of varying
styles for varying tastes. We cannot all admire Bach any
more than Barth. A concert made up entirely of fugues—
like a preacher who preaches only invitation sermons—
gives some credence to the definition of a fugue: "A piece
of music in which the voices come in one after another
and the audience go out one after another." For "audience"
substitute occasionally "congregation."

Why do we hold to the belief that in preaching all one

98

needs is one theme, one purpose, and one format? Why is this so peculiarly the preacher's myopia? Nowhere else do we strive to be so uninterestingly monotonous. Is it heresy to say that preaching to children and preaching to adults are two entirely different things? Well, it is to those who talk to the preacher and tell him how much they "enjoyed" the children's sermon. "To tell the truth, we really have to confess that usually we like it better than the other sermon." If a minister to whom this is either said or intimated, does not sit down with that comment and come to terms with it, he had better try selling another kind of insurance.

Even the message of the Bible is not the same to all ages. If it were not the most errant heresy, I should risk saying that I believe the Bible is an adult book—not for children at all. We do it and them an injustice by giving it to them in the same way in which we give it to their parents. What we want one age to believe about the Bible and about religion may not be at all what one should want another age to believe.

Radio and television coaches tell us that we ministers should not preach to a restricted audience, but should project our message in terms of a breadth of interest. A sermon directed at too specific a hearer will obviously be very much limited in its appeal and value to others. We need to remember this lesson—even in the pulpit of our church.

There is a very subtle form of singular coercion. Mr. Smith may be so dominant a personality that we see him before our eyes no matter where we look. He may turn out to be our local Sir Roger de Coverley, "landlord to the whole congregation." [4] Sir Roger happened to be a good landlord, but he might well be otherwise in our congregation.

The very next village is famous for the differences and contentions that rise between the parson and 'squire, who live in a perpetual state of war. The parson is always preaching at the 'squire; and the 'squire, to be revenged on the parson, never comes to church.[5]

Sir Roger exercises his rights in the choice of an incumbent for his parish: "A clergyman rather of plain sense than much learning, of a good aspect, a clear voice, a sociable temper, and, if possible, a man that understood a little of backgammon." Upon such a man he has settled an annuity for life and, "If he outlives me, he shall find that he was higher in my esteem than perhaps he thinks he is." It is hard—very hard—not to preach to a man like that. Good as he is—and Sir Roger de Coverley is by no means a bad man to have in one's church—one can so easily become a private chaplain to such a member, to the detriment of the other men and women who probably have a greater need of their minister's thought and attention. It would be so easy to write one's sermon in the study and be always conscious of our Sir Roger looking over our shoulder at what we have written. We should be less than human if we did not look up occasionally to see his approving nod when we have done well; but we should be more than human if we were to look up above him for the

[4] Joseph Addison, *The Spectator*, No. 112.
[5] *Ibid.*

approving nod of Another. Alas, if our Sir Roger turn out
to be Sir Oracle:

> Dress'd in an opinion
> Of wisdom, gravity, profound conceit;
> As who should say, "I am Sir Oracle,
> And when I ope my lips let no dog bark!" [6]

While reading Coleridge recently, I came upon this
statement of his made in July, 1833, one year before his
death at the age of sixty-two. He wrote, "When I was a
boy, I was fondest of Aeschylus; in youth and middle age
I preferred Euripides; now in my declining years I admire
Sophocles. I can now at length see that Sophocles is the
most perfect." How very revealing this remark is, and how
important to the preacher such an observation should be!
It could well help him toward an intelligent, sympathetic,
and so helpful ministry of preaching.

In the first place, all three Greek dramatists are writers
of tragedy. Horace Walpole wrote to Sir Horace Mann,
"The world is a comedy to those that think, a tragedy to
those who feel." Is this a suggestion of the great difference
between the sermon that is about theology and the one
that is about religion? Is it also a comment worthy of the
notice of those whose primary preoccupation is with what
and how we think? One of the great sentences in our English language was written by Philip Gosse to his son Edmund in what the latter was to call "the torment of the
postal inquisition." The father wrote in answer to his
son's letter expressing admiration for works of art, "You

[6] William Shakespeare, "The Merchant of Venice." Act I, scene 1.

may admire what is beautiful, so long as you do not become indifferent to what is wrong." [7]

Aeschylus, the youngest of the three, is given to lofty language and vivid imagery, even to the extent of approaching dangerously near bombast. How boys love that! His primary interest seems to have been in theology and religion, with their worlds of the ideal and the romantic. Human affairs throw light on their problems, which is certainly the relationship accepted by "youth." No wonder Coleridge "as a boy . . . was fond of Aeschylus." Aren't we all?

Euripides, his choice for youth and middle age, was the extreme opposite of Aeschylus. Unorthodox in his views, he showed strong strains of skepticism, with increasing doubt and uncertainty. His interests are on the human level, making what amounts to a psychological study of his characters. He is not predominantly interested in theology or in religion, but rather in ethical problems. The gods probably do exist, and are sometimes, somehow, and in some way helpful to man. Is it strange that Euripides, the young man of the three, should be the one to appeal to Coleridge the youth? Perhaps youth, with its philosophy and its idioms, does have something to say to youth.

Then comes age, the "declining years," named—someone has said—from the necessity to decline what we formerly accepted. With these years comes Sophocles. His was the consistent and firm approach to the problems of tragedy. While he held to the dignity, the worth, and the value of man, Sophocles held also to a mysterious and powerful force behind the universe whose powers and eternal laws

[7] Charteris, *op. cit.*, p. 17.

rule that earth. This is the power that is holy, even though it is, or perhaps even as it is, incomprehensible to men. Do we want a better appraisal of the latter years of man?

Here, then, is Coleridge, and each of us. The riddle of the Sphinx should be matched with the riddle of the Sermon: "What is it that laughs in the morning, frowns in the afternoon, and smiles at night?" Every preacher should be asked that question and should be required to know that the answer is the same as that for the Sphinx—man!

So we believe and so we preach!

Chapter VII

To Serve a Cause

It is a mistake not to take one's task seriously; to take oneself seriously is equally a mistake. It is wisdom to distinguish between the two. George Hedley, in his striking book *The Superstitions of the Irreligious,* says very truly:

They who are the surest of their religious foundation are the most readily able to be gay about it. The Catholics and Jews, taking their faith for granted and never doubting its ultimate validity, delight to tell stories about the foibles both of their clergy and of their laymen. Some other groups, *per contra,* by their very sensitivity to ridicule announce their deep-rooted doubts of their own position. He who has confidence in himself can afford to laugh at himself. He who has confidence in his religious values can afford to be gay about them, because he is fundamentally happy within them.[1]

We have quoted Johnson earlier as saying, "Almost all absurdity of conduct arises from the imitation of those whom we cannot resemble." We were talking then about our confusion arising out of our comparison with others. Now we use it to indicate the need for recognizing our limitations in another area. There is just so much we can

[1] (New York: The Macmillan Co., 1951) , p. 134. Used by permission of the publisher.

do, no matter who we are; just so much we can achieve, no matter how long or how expertly we labor. Then we must stop—stop worrying, especially. A recent book *The Arts of Living,* edited by Gilbert Highet, has two contributors who must be read at this point. Jean Stafford writes on "The Art of Accepting Oneself" and Emily Kimbrough discusses "The Art of Using What You Have." How true! There is an acknowledged sacrament in work. *Laborare est orare,* to be sure. There is too often an unacknowledged sacrament in rest, although the Sabbath tradition should have taught us otherwise.

We ought to work hard and incessantly; there is generally no substitute for toil. But it is no disgrace to stop working when we know we have done all we can do, just as it is no evidence of weakening when we pray that God will bless our labors. It is simply that we must learn the difference between letting God do it and letting God finish it. Not even Jesus was *completely* successful; there was still a twelfth disciple to mar the record. "I kept them in thy name which thou hast given me; I have guarded them, and none of them is lost but the son of perdition." (John 17:12.) Even if the phrase that follows, "that the scripture might be fulfilled," be taken to be other than a part of the entire Fourth Gospel redaction, it still remains a factor against the full success of Jesus' labors. There is further evidence of the limitations of his ministry in such incidents as those recorded in Matt. 13:58, Mark 6:5, and Luke 4:29, to cite a few.

Oliver Wendell Holmes in *Over the Teacups* put it frankly and forcefully:

The Jews are with us as a perpetual lesson to teach us modesty and civility. The religion we profess is not self-evident. It did not convince the people to whom it was sent. We have no claim to take it for granted that we are all right, and they are all wrong. And, therefore, in the midst of all the triumphs of Christianity, it is well that the stately synagogue should lift its walls by the side of the aspiring cathedral, a perpetual reminder that there are many mansions in the Father's earthly house as well as in the heavenly one; that civilized humanity, longer in time and broader in space than any historical form of belief, is mightier than any one institution or organization it includes.

The good Doctor's use of this historical fact is well within the purview of our present purpose. It adds the necessary virtues of a consequent humility and civility.

How well Jesus could talk of a condition easily observable during a walk through the countryside, but one apparently unnoticed as also being within mankind: there are at least four kinds of ground into which the properly sown seed of the well-meaning sower may fall. And let us declare at the outset that there is no justification for saying that the good ground is even as much as one-fourth of the whole. This is agriculture, not mathematics, that the master is teaching.

Others, too, have made the observation and have set bounds and limits to a man's achievable horizon. I stood one day on the shore throwing stones in an attempt to have them land on a thin strip of land only a short distance from where I stood. Try as I might, I could not make one throw reach its mark. A much older man standing by my side finally remarked quietly, "Man has his limits, hasn't he?" Heaven may be the reason for a man's reach exceeding his grasp, but it does not remove the disparagement between the two. Galsworthy in his *Candelabra* reminds us that there are two kinds of men:

As truly as that oil and water do not mix, there are two kinds of men. The main cleavage in the whole tale of life is this subtle, all-pervading division of mankind into the man of facts and the man of feeling. And not by what they are or do can they be told one from the other, but just by their attitude toward finality.

Coleridge calls our attention to the fact that there is a predetermined futility to some of our efforts:

Talk to a blind man—he knows he wants the sense of sight, and willingly makes the proper allowances. But there are certain internal senses which a man may want, and yet be wholly ignorant that he wants them. It is most unpleasant to converse with such persons on subjects of taste, philosophy, or religion. Of course, there is no reasoning with them, for they do not possess the facts, on which the reasoning must be grounded. Nothing is possible but a naked dissent, which implies a sort of unsocial contempt; or —what a man of kind disposition is very likely to fall into—a heartless tacit acquiescence, which borders too nearly on duplicity.[2]

Lost causes have a basic romantic quality that often makes one utter the words with a verbal halo attached to them. It is well to accept them as such if that is absolutely necessary; evasion of a "lost" cause may be only an error of judgment produced by rendering a verdict on inade-

[2] *Notebooks,* 1812.

quate evidence or upon hasty conclusions. More seriously, it may be the gratuitous assumption of martyrdom that is both unnecessary and also a little tarnished. Just because I am engaged in a cause that others consider lost is no proof that they are either stupid or wrong:

> For O, to some
> Not to be martyrs is a martyrdom.[3]

When all that, and more, has been said, much yet remains to be urged why we ought not to avoid alignment with causes both lost and unpopular. Success in a cause is less important than the cause itself. To be a part of a noble cause that will be lost is better than to be a leader of an ignoble cause that succeeds. "Better fifty years of Europe than a cycle of Cathay" was written by one who "held it better men should perish one by one, than that earth should stand at gaze like Joshua's moon in Ajalon!" [4] Van Wyck Brooks well wrote, "The intellectual man, if he follows his instincts, will always throw what weight he has on the side of 'lost causes, and forsaken beliefs, and unpopular names, and impossible loyalties.' " Of course he was quoting from that famous utterance of Arnold regarding the character of Oxford University. And he adds, "A writer is important not by the amount of territory he enters or claims, but by the amount he colonizes." [5]

At this point I want to make a plea for an acceptance of what an English writer has called "A Forgotten Sacrament,"

[3] John Donne, "Litany."
[4] Alfred Lord Tennyson, "Locksley Hall."
[5] Brooks, *Opinions of Oliver Allston*, pp. 278-79, 297.

but first, and by way of preparation for both the understanding and the acceptance of the sacrament, let us consider the fact of just how much of the success of preaching is due to the preacher. We have already said enough to indicate what we may expect to be the truth.

A preacher, just as any man in any situation, is limited by what he truly is. "Which of you by being anxious can add one cubit to his span of life?" (Matt. 6:27.) Neither can he by being anxious or in any other way develop himself beyond the limits already set by his precise being. A man cannot change the color of his eyes or the skeletal formation of his body. The former is in the genes, the latter is as rigid as the bones that compose it. So, also, is much of a man's native equipment—or lack of it. He does well to learn precisely what he is and then be superb within his definitions. We have also indicated the disturbing, but ultimately revealing, truth that the congregation is a predetermined factor in the success or failure of any sermon. Indeed, let us clearly state and definitely agree that a sermon is not what a man puts on paper, nor is it what he says to his congregation on Sunday morning. The sermon, let it always be remembered, is what takes place in the minds and lives of its hearers!

Finally, however, the most important factor in preaching is the one that makes the whole matter a religious act. Up to this point we have been talking about preaching precisely as we should have about any other form of public speech—the lecture, the after-dinner address, the monologue. But this is a sermon and this is preaching, which means basically that God is present in the act. Leave God out and it is neither a sermon nor preaching.

Daniel Day Williams, writing about *What Present-Day Theologians Are Thinking,* says:

In a book on preaching entitled *The Servant of the Word,* H. H. Farmer has stressed the personal relationship in the encounter between God and man. He interprets the event of preaching as one way in which the encounter may take place. ... the center of attention is upon that for which the minister himself is listening in his preparation and his utterance, when he is given the grace to listen, that is God's word of judgment and reconciliation for this man and this congregation here and now.[6]

This, we preachers must never forget nor neglect. We must say not only to those who ask, but we must repeat it constantly to our own questing and questioning spirit: "Wist ye not that I must be about my Father's business?" (Luke 2:49.)

So to the forgotten sacrament. It is the title of a chapter in an earlier book by John Oman, *Vision and Authority.*

Though God, from a tender regard to the spirits of His children made in His own image with this power of free choice of good or evil, endures much resistance to His will and confusion in His world, His servant is not always able to escape the temptation to be peremptory when he has power and hysterical when he lacks it. The sense of responsibility in face of the sad estrangement from God of the souls he cannot convince, and of the narrow limits of any aid one soul can give another, has often led to hard antagonism and hurtful insistence. ...

Our Lord knew this danger which beset His followers. He

[6] (New York: Harper & Bros., 1952), p. 135.

knew not only the hastiness of human nature, but the earnestness He Himself had inspired which calls man to endurance, the humility which would be ready to accept blame for failure, and the devotion which might persist, not merely to the useless sacrifice of life, but to the sadder loss of faith. Therefore, He not only warned His disciples against this kind of resistance of evil, but safeguarded them by a sacrament of failure. . . .

But when He instructed them to shake off solemnly the dust from their shoes as a testimony and to depart from the place where they had delivered their message and it had not been received, He went further, and taught them that the final responsibility even for overcoming evil with good was not theirs. . . .

To her great loss the Church seems to have forgotten it. Yet the Master appointed for it a solemn and impressive symbol when first He sent forth His servants to their work in the world. . . .

Perhaps, even in His life of superhuman thoughtfulness and care for others, there is no more striking instance of His consideration for the limitations of our nature, and His Divine prevision of our greatest dangers.[7]

Now to go back for just a brief moment to causes—lost or otherwise—that still have in them the redeeming quality of nobility and dignity. Like every other minister I have fought in causes that were doomed, perhaps even destined, to be lost. I, too, believed they were noble and worthy of any sacrifice; and I hoped, though I was not always too sure, that I had a foeman worthy of my steel. In more mature moments I have prayed that my own blade might be worthy of the cause. That makes a difference. To begin

[7] Used by permission of the publishers, Hodder & Stoughton, Ltd., London, and Harper & Bros., New York.

with one's self, one's sword, one's foe, is not nearly so satisfactory, nor so ultimately rewarding, as to begin with one's Cause. Once determine the worthiness of that, and we have a reward in the mere fact that we are part of such a contest.

Perhaps it is entirely too self-satisfying, but I respond wholeheartedly to the classic St. Crispian's Day speech of *Henry V*—call it idealism, romanticism, or what you will. Make it a matter of Elizabethan fustian or theatrical bombast; it will not lose its truth for all you strip it of its glamor. King Henry has found the heart of all true satisfaction and of honor—to be a fighter in a great cause. He even goes so far as to deny the Earl of Westmoreland's wish that they had with them for this field of Agincourt "but one ten thousand of those men in England that do no work today" by declaring, "The fewer men, the greater share of honour." Moreover, if there be one who "hath no stomach to this fight, let him depart. . . ."

> We would not die in that man's company
> That fears his fellowship to die with us.
> This day is call'd the feast of Crispian:
> He that outlives this day, and comes safe home,
> Will stand a tip-toe when this day is named,
> And rouse him at the name of Crispian.

He will live always in the pride of having fought this noble battle.

> And gentlemen in England now a-bed
> Shall think themselves accursed they were not here;

And hold their manhoods cheap whiles any speak
That fought with us upon Saint Crispin's day.[8]

Is there a reward for fighting at Agincourt—so long as
there is a St. Crispian's Day? Is there a reward for preaching
the gospel of Jesus Christ so long as there is a Christmas
Day or an Easter Day?

Somewhere Robert Louis Stevenson says that sooner or
later we all sit down to a banquet of consequences. How
true! The banquet is part of our daily judgment already
referred to. We have to eat; our only choice is what we shall
eat, and our only possible choices are what is set before us.
The Lord may prepare a table before us in the presence
of our enemies, but the "banquet of consequences" is
provided from our own larder, and may not be so pleasant.
It often becomes more nearly what Edwin Arlington
Robinson calls, "The bread that every man must eat
alone." [9] We talk cautiously about the "rewards" of the
ministry and of preaching, but not because there is none.
Rather we want to be discriminating and justified when
we say, "This is our reward." We wish to be very sure that
we do not fall into the company of those surprised—and
self-cheated—persons who labor strenuously and pains-
takingly at worthy tasks, but by reason of their unworthy
and inadequate reasons and goals, arrive at a success and
a payment that are strangely marred by the judgment,
"They have their reward," or as Phillips translates it:
"Believe me, they have had all the reward they are going
to get" (Matt. 6:2). Instead of being a word of congratu-
lation, it becomes a revelation of the incomplete.

[8] Act IV, scene 3.
[9] "The Man Against the Sky."

Quite some time ago I saw this advertisement in a newspaper under the "Personal" heading:

> CHRISTIAN man wanted. Strong, or with car, to carry portable amplifier to streets & squares on Sundays, and, who would help to preach the Gospel. No compensation.

Of course he meant "no money," certainly not "no returns." Yet many would say that both were true, and many more would be unwilling to venture the statement that they are not true. Low salaries and curtailed incomes are probably the lot of the minister. And what else does he get out of it except what he can compel himself to believe are the true riches? Is not a preacher's reward so obviously nonmaterial that we sometimes succumb to the belief that it must also be immaterial? Are we not, in our plea for the compensation of the ministry, often merely rationalizing our losses and glorifying our substitutes? The workman is still worthy of his food (Matt. 10:10), and we still need more than the mere poetry of the injunction against muzzling the ox when he is treading out the grain (Deut. 25:4). The subject is a well-explored and well-exploited one and need not detain us unduly. Besides it is not always in our power to change or control its provision for our maintenance. We had better employ our time in an area where we do have almost complete jurisdiction. We may determine the satisfactions of our souls; we may alert our minds to a sensitiveness that reveals our "compensations." And there are compensations—gloriously undeniable ones!

Some of them are very obvious, both to the minister and to his people. Others are the secret of the minister

114

alone, hardly even guessed at by any other. These are the secrets—the compensations, that come quietly to him when he sits down with himself and summons the ghost of Yesterday to show impartially what store he has laid by. In that store will always be treasures of the mind and soul —his mind and soul as well as the mind and soul of others. Let us begin with one of the less obvious compensations of preaching.

We make much of the fact that a man's sermons are a reflection of his life and character—and so we should. It could not well be otherwise. We ought equally to emphasize that they are also the creator of the man. One hardly needs to argue the fact that a stream never rises higher than its source, that out of the abundance of the heart the mouth speaketh, and much else that asserts how much we can see of the man in his creation. It becomes necessary to see also that if the sermon—or any created work of art—is the legitimate brain child of the man; and it is equally true that "the child is father to the man." Having created the sermon, the minister does not thereby send it from him merely to do his will, to be remembered by those who hear it (if happily they do), to be perhaps conveniently forgotten by him in an expression of humility. Far from it! The bread that is cast upon the waters still returns, after many or very many days, and it returns to the one who cast it.

Thus T. S. Eliot writes that, of course, an author gives some bit of himself to his characters, but

on the other hand, a character which succeeds in interesting its author may elicit from the author latent potentialities of his own being. I believe that the author imparts something of himself to his characters, but I also believe that he is influenced by the characters he creates.[10]

And so do I. How carefully, then, we must prepare our sermons, for they are not only our creations, but our creators. The thoughts, the beliefs, the proposals we hold, make, and urge upon others have a subtle way of urging themselves upon us. If we continue to preach caustically or carpingly, we need not possibly expect to develop within ourselves a spirit of tolerance or humility. Men become like the gods they worship; they also become like the God they preach.

There are some things I cannot preach, now or ever. Oh, perhaps I can say them, but I cannot preach them. They deal with those things about which life has taught me and which there is no possibility of my forgetting. They are in the areas of thought and life where I am a total stranger, without even a passport that entitles me to visit them. Some are in countries that I have deliberately crossed off my map of interest and inquiry. For me they will ever be a part of that vast Terra Incognita which we may even come to respect. Yet having said that there is a large amount of territory that I cannot touch with my preaching now, I fight to do so—I must fight to do so. It is in that fighting to create such sermons that I find that they have also created me. Just as flexing the muscles of the body to do a task creates muscles to do it, so exercising the fibers of

[10] "The Three Voices of Poetry," *Atlantic Monthly*, April, 1954, p. 40. Used by permission.

the soul to speak effectively creates the fibers themselves. Think of the times when, in our own preaching, we have come to know with disturbing clarity the meaning of the advice about offering our gift when we had aught against our brother. How often we have had to make that stubborn journey back to our brother before we could lay upon our pulpit an offering to the Lord! This became no mere injunction from a far-off age; it was a haunting specter of our own endangered soul. The sermon we would preach became the sermon that first preached itself to us, then made us obey it ourselves before we could preach it to others. So we became like the sermon we did preach. As a man about to play the part of Christus in a Passion Play, the minister prepares himself to give real effectiveness to his part, and finds that he has acquired an effective reality within himself. This is one of the most assured and approved compensations of the ministry of preaching.

It seems hardly necessary to say again that there is still a demand for example as well as precept, or that there is a constant unwillingness to accept the words of those "ungracious pastors" who show us "the steep and thorny way to heaven" while they themselves "the primrose path of dalliance" tread. Such a one who "recks not his own rede" is no more likely to convince Miss America than Ophelia. A right-minded preacher is fully aware of this danger and, if for no other reason, seeks to provide his precept with an example. Perhaps no other form of clerical and lay weakness has been so exploited as the basis for the rejection of Christianity, as this observed disparagement. It is still true that "the greatest cause of infidelity is the misrepresentation of Christianity by so-called Christians," as Charles Torrey wrote years ago. (He very probably was but paraphrasing the ages.) The preacher, being so forewarned, is often forearmed as well.

The result of his unwillingness to contribute the slightest added hindrance to Christian acceptance is his own particular form of decision to eat no meat if meat cause his brother to stumble. This is at least as often a motive and a power for the good life as any fear lest saving others, he may himself be rejected. Let it be remembered that Paul said both things.

Yes, like priest, like people—and like people, like priest; but also like sermons, like preacher! It still seems happily true that the miracle of healing may occur to a man "as he (is) going in the way."

Most people have to make the decision to follow Christ; the preacher has already made that decision. He has publicly announced it by his assumption of the divine office of minister. He has proclaimed, by his ordination, that he professes to speak both in behalf of and in the place of God. He has committed himself irrevocably to at least pronouncements of the Way of Life. Sooner or later it dawns upon him that he has also committed himself to walk that same way. He may, in truth, echo both Portia's divine and his own nature when she exclaims, "It is a good divine that follows his own instructions: I can easier tell twenty what were good to be done, than be one of the twenty to follow mine own teaching." He may echo them, but he dare not illustrate them. His condemnation is that he must walk with conviction when he is somewhat lacking in assurance; it is his glory that only so can he fully preach the conviction, and even approximately achieve it for himself.

One final and brief word about another reward for being a minister and a preacher—a subtle word that is in the vocabulary only of those who believe because they have experienced the inarticulate. This is a word used only by those who are repaid by the smiles of old folks and the laughter of young ones; by the light that shines behind the eyes of a friend; by the return of the lifeblood to the pallid face of a weary, disillusioned, and frustrated man or defeated woman; by the new strength in the handclasp of one who is leaving to go on rather than to go back; this is a word only for such as know these.

The Confidential Clerk of T. S. Eliot is Colby Simpkins, a young man of hidden truths and unsuspected relationships. His new employer, Sir Claude Mulhammer, tells him that he, Sir Claude, always wanted to be a potter, because he loved to shape things; he loved form and color, and he loved the material that the potter handles. But he soon came to know beyond question that he would not become a first-rate potter. This was beyond his capabilities. And could a man ever be said "to have a vocation to be a second-rate potter?" That realization brought all the unsatisfied longings to be worthwhile, all the unfulfilled aspirations to be an artist. He knew the fears that he was only an inept and clumsy workman, never to be a craftsman; a copier never a creator; only a reproducer of other men's glories. But, he says, he also understood something of this in Colby, who is a musician. He will get him a piano, one of the best. And, he adds:

THE MAN WHO WOULD PREACH

When you are alone at your piano, in the evening,
I believe you will go through the private door
Into the real world, as I do, sometimes.

The reply of Colby is the subtle word of life's compensation to the sincere and dedicated soul, however inadequate and ineffective it feels.

                      I know
I should never have become a great organist,
As I aspired to be. I'm not an executant;
I'm only a shadow of the great composers.
Always, when I play to myself,
I hear the music I should like to have written,
As the composer heard it when it came to him;
But when I played before other people
I was always conscious that what *they* heard
Was not what I hear when I play to myself.
What I hear is a great musician's music,
What they hear is an inferior rendering.[11]

[11] Used by permission of the publishers, Harcourt, Brace & Co.

I Am a Minister

There recently came to my attention an illustration in an old book. The book was *Margarita Philosophica*, written by Gregorious Reisch and published in 1503; the illustration was entitled "The Tower of Learning." It presented the general scheme of education from the old Roman days down to the time of Shakespeare, and even beyond. The tower stands in the right foreground, and just to the left is a young boy about to enter it. Admitting him to the tower is a young woman opening the door with the key of grammar, while she extends to him a hornbook from which he is to learn his letters.

On the first two floors of the tower the child is taught Latin; the third floor is for arithmetic, rhetoric, and logic; he learns astronomy, geometry, and music on the fourth floor; the fifth floor introduces him to moral philosophy and natural philosophy. The tower is capped by theology —the queen of the sciences. His respective teachers are Donatus, Priscian, Boethius, Cicero, Aristotle, Ptolemy, Euclid, Pythagoras, Seneca, Pliny, and Peter Lombard. What an array of subjects and what an academy of teachers! And theology has the highest place!

How far we have come since that sixteenth century to a day when our order is more like the facetiously ascribed arrangement of sons in the British family: the eldest son goes into the government; the next son into the law; the third son into business; and the youngest son, poor fellow, enters the church. Perhaps the Rev. G. W. Streatfield in *Between the Acts* by Virginia Woolf is what many or most folks have in mind when they think of the minister. Miss Woolf characterizes him as ". . . a piece of traditional church-furniture; a corner cupboard, or the top beam of a gate, fashioned by generations of village carpenters after some lost-in-the-mists-of-antiquity model." Certainly we ministers have lost much of the sincere and genuine approval given to our position by those of other days and other times. Here and there we are met with a straight-forward acceptance and are cheered by the simplicity of those who regard us with an acceptable reverence that sees not ourselves, but our associations. There is a subtle confirmation of the general change in attitude toward us in the intuitive way we come to recognize at once the unctuous use of "Reverend" or the irresponsible bestowing of "Doctor" upon us by those who have neither discernment nor power.

The external causes of this depreciation of religion and its consequent loss of prestige are not difficult to discover. It would seem unnecessary to do more than merely point out the rapid growth of the secular world, the area of human life that is apparently outside the interests of, and unrelated to, the world of religion. If religion has retreated within itself, that is all the more reason for an accentuated difference. Most people will consider it merely an axiom that religion and the church have utterly failed to make commensurate progress within their own fields. So to do has only aggravated the injury to the cause of religion.

Moreover, education in the interest of religion has been lamentably behind secular education. The latter has increased in power and in scope, while the former has not as yet even established itself beyond the limits laid out for it by a comparatively few farseeing and hopeful adventurers. We require elementary education in the schools and we are rapidly subsidizing education in the colleges and universities; we are still arguing even the character of education in the churches. If we of the church could be a little more objective about the situation, we should see more clearly what is involved.

All this would be little more than trying to set fire to an already burned-over field if it were not for its relation to another and far more serious defection. It is bad enough that the condition exists, but it is worse that the minister has accepted it meekly and allowed it to influence and color his attitude toward himself and his ministry. The uncomfortable fact is that the ministry has lost its sense of dignity. The minister has acquiesced in the general conspiracy to rob him of his authority. Worst of all, the determinating and absolutely requisite sense of mission has deteriorated into a humiliating experience of being little more than a modern Ruth "amid the alien corn."

As if this were not bad enough, we go on to greater devastations of mood and spirit. We are enervated by our concern for the growing weakness of the institution we serve—the church. It seems of little worth to be throwing away our lives in the interests of a social organization that is moribund. Gradually we begin to doubt even the cause that has hitherto loomed before us like some chalice of ancient knighthood. But the end, in every sense of the word, comes when we lose sight of the very object of our service—God. This is the final degradation of the ministry.

But if the stream of influence goes in this one direction, it goes in the opposite direction as well. The church, the cause, and God are accepted by the world at the valuation we place upon them. By placing a low estimate upon them, by doubting their efficiency—or even their reality—we need not be surprised when the world outside ourselves places a similarly dubious interpretation upon them. Let a businessman mark down the price of an article he has for sale, and many will believe that he is trying to sell a damaged article. Many others will question whether the re-marked article is the same as that originally offered for a higher price.

Our recourse seems often to be found in an attempt to substitute for our former high sense of value, the new criteria of the world. So we talk about the size of the church we serve, and the number of additions we have made to its membership in the course of a year. We boast of our standing in the community and the number of addresses we have been called upon to deliver, the number of invocations we have offered, in the pursuance of our extracurricular activities. We judge our fellow ministers by their salaries in the same way that we feel we have made progress when our own salary is raised or when we move to a "bigger" church, where the word always means more members and more salary. The church budget is not to be slighted or allowed to go unrecognized and unappreciated; it goes down in the cold print of the association and convention reports and so uncontestably states our position and importance. I have known some ministers who were more concerned to have us know that they had a secretary than that they had a gospel.

It is time we put a stop to all this. It is high time we took a decided stand against this wave of depreciation. Listen to Paul as he tells his readers in Rome that he has a serious work to do. Listen to him especially as he says, "I magnify mine office." Some of our modern translators have given to this declaration a power that should bring us up with a start of guilt. "I make the most of my ministry" (Goodspeed) ; "I lay great stress on my office" (Moffatt) ; "I take pride in my ministry" (Weymouth) ; "I magnify my ministry" (Revised Standard Version) . That is the way a minister should talk. That is the fearless and confident assertion he should make about the work he earlier chose as the most tremendous challenge he knew. Here is no vestige of capitulation to a current mood of despair or imputation of inferiority. Here is the ringing challenge he flings back, not because he is ignorant of the inadequacies within himself or the difficulties of his undertaking, but because he accepts them as imperious demands that he put the burden of responsibility squarely where it belongs.

Both the church and the world are in desperate need of ministers of religion who have great confidence in themselves, in the church and in their God, men in whom the light of faith burns steadily and clearly. Such ministers will serve not only the church, but other ministers as well. Enthusiasm and faith are just as contagious and just as empowering as despair and doubt. We have a duty to ourselves, to our church, to our cause, to our God, and to our fellow ministers.

This deep and earnest longing for a restoration of a proud and confident ministry is well expressed by a "Returned Chaplain" who wrote "Why I Gave Up My Congregation" in the March, 1948, number of *Commentary,* a publication of the American Jewish Committee.

They [the rabbis] are adept in political and literary discussion and engage in such discussion very freely. I have heard God justified by social theories, the Bible praised on literary merit, Jewish traditions historicized. But I have rarely encountered a simple and complete acceptance of Jewishness that needs no rationalizing. I have found almost no sign of that prophetic zeal which such acceptance—and only such acceptance—can call forth.

In brief, I have found talented rabbis, but not rabbinic rabbis. The rabbis, while they may be a powerful influence in the life of the community, have no acceptance in the community as rabbis. They carry weight in all fields where, whatever their rights as men, they have no claim from the standpoint of their life's vocation. . . .

I hear the same talk that I heard before I left. Talk about "enjoyable" services, "satisfying" sermons, "inspiring" synagogues. I hear discussions about the choice of English reading, the separation or non-separation of pews. I see a determined effort to make the synagogue "attractive," as if through some aesthetic magic we could somehow draw in the spiritually inert without having to disturb their inertia. The road must be made easier; the rabbi must draw the indifferent into the synagogue, even if, in the process, the synagogue must be emptied of its meaning and the rabbi voided of his rabbinate.[1]

In the true community the author envisions the rabbi

[1] Vol. 5, No. 3, pp. 235-36. The quotation in the following paragraph is from the same essay, p. 237. These quotations are used by permission of the publisher.

"would find himself at last able to speak in his own idiom, as a complete and self-respecting personality rooted in a deep and old history, and he would no longer have to compete with the theater in pageantry, with the latest best-seller in literary modishness, with the nearest church in ritual appeal. He would serve a community that truly needed a rabbi."

Allow for the obvious titular changes, and you will not need to make one word different to express the equally fervent prayer of every Christian minister who lays great stress on his office, who takes pride in his ministry. I think of my father's mild, yet most effective, rebuke to me when I told him I had answered my schoolteacher's query about his occupation by saying, "He is a publisher." "I am not a publisher," corrected my father with a humility that bespoke a genuine pride, "I am a printer." Then he added significantly, "Benjamin Franklin was a printer, too."

I am a minister.
I believe in the ministry.
When the time came to choose what I should do with my
    life, where I should serve mankind,
I chose the church.
When all the ways of being a useful man lay open before
    me,
When the world offered many roads I might travel,
I chose the path of Christian service.
It was not the only way; I chose it out of countless others.
It was my answer to a question that was asked by some-
    thing deep within me.
And there was another Questioner, from somewhere out-
    side myself, and high above me.
That other Questioner I believed was God.

THE MAN WHO WOULD PREACH

I still believe it.
And so I chose the ministry.
I am a minister.
I believe in the ministry.

The years have past, few or many,
According as I think of whether they belonged to me
Or to that other Questioner.
A countless host of other folk afforded me a fellowship
    that I could see and happily enjoy.
But there was, too, another fellowship I only felt and
    knew, and counted on.
The road I walked was thronged with many—pilgrims like
    myself.
Some walked with sturdy step that challenged me to be
    at least as sure as they.
Some, lamed at birth or later by some accident,
Slowed my step and loosed my tongue.
There were many quite heedless of my presence along the
    very road they walked themselves;
But there were also those who looked at me—
Shyly, hopefully, challengingly.
If ever I spoke a helpful word, I spoke it,
Humbly and prayerfully, to these.
Often I doubted, often I was anxious,
Often I knew the aching bitterness of real defeat.
But often I was lifted up beyond myself and all my cares,
By some soft murmured word or soul-relieving sigh, scarcely
    heard.
I was a minister.

I am a minister.
I magnify my ministry.
I lay great stress upon my office.
I take pride in my ministry.

9 781258 348373